God's Superheroes

God's Superheroes

Amazing Catholic Men

Mary Fluhr Bajda

Our Sunday Visitor
Huntington, Indiana

Nihil Obstat
Msgr. Michael Heintz, Ph.D.
Censor Librorum

Imprimatur
✠ Kevin C. Rhoades
Bishop of Fort Wayne-South Bend
July 21, 2021

The *Nihil Obstat* and *Imprimatur* are official declarations that a book is free from doctrinal or moral error. It is not implied that those who have granted the *Nihil Obstat* and *Imprimatur* agree with the contents, opinions, or statements expressed.

Except where noted, the Scripture citations used in this work are taken from the *Revised Standard Version of the Bible—Second Catholic Edition* (Ignatius Edition), copyright © 1965, 1966, 2006 National Council of the Churches of Christ in the United States of America. Used by permission. All rights reserved.

Every reasonable effort has been made to determine copyright holders of excerpted materials and to secure permissions as needed. If any copyrighted materials have been inadvertently used in this work without proper credit being given in one form or another, please notify Our Sunday Visitor in writing so that future printings of this work may be corrected accordingly.

Our Sunday Visitor Publishing Division, Our Sunday Visitor, Inc., 200 Noll Plaza, Huntington, IN 46750; 1-800-348-2440; www.osv.com.

ISBN: 978-1-68192-636-0 (Inventory No. T2496)
eISBN: 978-1-68192-637-7

1. JUVENILE NONFICTION—Biography & Autobiography.
2. RELIGION—Christianity—Saints & Sainthood.
3. RELIGION—Christianity—Catholic.

LCCN: 2021942895

Cover design: Tyler Ottinger
Cover art: Melinda Steffen
Interior design: Amanda Falk
Interior art: Melinda Steffen

PRINTED IN THE UNITED STATES OF AMERICA

For my greatest blessings:
my loving husband, Jimi,
and my wonderful children James, Evangeline, and Isabelle.

And for my parents, George and Carmen Fluhr,
who gave me this beautiful Catholic faith!

And for you, my readers, the next generation of God's superheroes.
May you accept your mission and go light your world!

"God would never inspire me with desires which cannot be
realized, so in spite of my littleness, I can hope to be a saint."

— Saint Thérèse, The Little Flower

POPE EMERITUS BENEDICT XVI SAID:
"The ways of the Lord are not easy, but we were not created for an easy life, but for great things, for goodness."

TABLE OF CONTENTS

INTRODUCTION

Superheroes are everywhere — in the movies, on television, in video games. It's exciting to imagine these extraordinary people with amazing powers who fight evil, save people, and are a force for good in the world. Every superhero has an origin story. Most of them start as regular, ordinary people. Then something happens to change them (radioactive spider bite, genetic mutation, ancient power-giving artifact, traumatic event, or something else). Once they have these powers, the choice is before them. Do they selflessly fight for the good or seek personal gain and power? If they choose good, they become superheroes and go out into the world to help people, fight evil, and give hope.

Did you know that God has superheroes of his own? Some were teachers, doctors, activists, television personalities, writers, mountain climbers, and musicians. Some were troublemakers, practical jokers, partiers, and rebels. They started as ordinary people. Then they encountered God, and they changed. They went out to the world with courage and determination. They stood against evil and injustice and made a difference. Some of them even had what could be called "superpowers." God gave them special abilities that helped them bring people to God.

God's superheroes are still champions for good today. They are sending you a call to action and want you to stand in their place. They want to help you find the mission that God has for you. They want to inspire you to step forward and become what God made you to be. They want to be friends for your journey through this crazy, wonderful, sometimes really difficult life. These are their stories. Get to know them. They want to stand by your side in every adventure you go on and against the obstacles you fight. They want to help you become one of God's superheroes too!

IN CASE YOU WERE WONDERING...

While everyone who goes to heaven is a saint (that's what the word *saint* means), sometimes there is a person who was such an exceptional example of following Christ that the Church decides to issue a formal declaration saying that person is a saint in heaven. This declaration is called canonization.

What does it take to be declared a saint? The person has to live an admirable Catholic life spreading justice, peace, and love, as God calls each of us to do. Or the person can die as a martyr, defending the Faith to the very end by words and actions. Either way will get you to heaven! To be actually declared a saint, though, the person has to go through the Church's process of canonization, which has four steps.

Usually, the process does not begin until at least five years after the holy person's death. This gives the Church time to see if the influence and reputation of the person grows and spreads, or fades and disappears. After this time, if there is still a great devotion and respect for this person, an official cause for canonization is opened in their name. From that time on, the person is referred to as a **Servant of God**.

Once the cause is opened, the Servant of God's life is carefully examined. Church officials interview witnesses, study the person's writings, and look at the person's entire life to make sure that they lived a truly holy life. After a thorough investigation, if the officials determine that this person truly is an inspiring example, then the pope will declare that person to be **Venerable**.

The next step requires evidence of a miracle of God that happened because the Venerable was prayed to and asked for their help and intercession (that they would pray to God for a specific purpose). This is most often sudden, physical healing. The Church carefully examines every claim of a miracle using doctors and scientists (including some that aren't Catholic) to make sure that there is no possible natural explanation. Once one miracle is confirmed, the person is declared **Blessed** by the pope.

When a second miracle is confirmed, using the same strict method of verification, the pope declares the Blessed a **Saint,** and he or she is given a special feast day on the Church Calendar.

The Church wants to make sure that the people we look up to as saints are the truest examples of holiness, so that we can, by imitating them, become holy. Ask God to help you find your mission, and then live your life, just as Jesus would want you to. You, too, can become a saint!

1
MIGUEL

Master of Disguise

*A daring, guitar-playing jokester who became
a Master of Disguise to help people, to protect
the Faith, and to inspire a nation.*

Miguel Pro was born in Guadalupe, Mexico, in 1891. He was a happy child with a lot of mischievous energy, but was also prone to injuries and illnesses. Once, he was unconscious for a long time only to open his eyes and, with a big smile, immediately ask for some cocol — his favorite Mexican sweet bread.

As he grew older, Miguel's sense of humor and rebellious streak often got him into trouble. He tormented his teacher with a lizard. He walked into a total stranger's house with his sister and told the owner that they were there to buy some really ugly art that was on the wall. He stole a visiting priest's vestments and gave some very interesting "sermons." One evening, he almost fell off the roof of his house, which caused a pack of forbidden cigarettes to spill out of his pocket down into his father's horrified face. He loved to play practical jokes and would take any dare. An avid guitar player and singer, Miguel also liked to make people laugh by imitating the voices and mannerisms of family and friends.

The teenaged Miguel wandered into a church and heard a sermon about Jesus' crucifixion.

> **MIGUEL SAID:**
> "I see God's hand so palpably in everything that almost — almost I fear they won't kill me in these adventures. That will be a fiasco for me, who sighs to go to heaven and start tossing off arpeggios on the guitar with my guardian angel."

After talking about all that Jesus had endured and suffered for us, the priest pointed at the crucifix and said, "All this Christ did and suffered for us, and what are we doing for him?" Miguel felt those words hit him like a ton of bricks. What had he done for Christ? Those words haunted him, and he finally accepted the challenge by entering a Jesuit seminary at the age of twenty.

At the time Miguel became a priest, the Catholic Faith was being persecuted by the Mexican government. Being Catholic, attending Mass, and receiving the sacraments were all against the law, and punishable by imprisonment or worse. The churches were closed and the priests were in hiding. This is when Miguel's daring spirit and acting ability came into play. He joined a group of Catholics known as the *cristeros*, soldiers for Christ, who were committed to defending the Faith. Since the local authorities were always on guard against any priest trying to spread the Faith, Miguel became a master of disguise to help his people. In rags like a beggar, he would come in the night to say Mass or perform a marriage. Dressed as a street sweeper, he would stop into a local house to hear confessions and baptize babies. In a policeman's uniform, he would brazenly walk straight into the jail to give holy Communion to prisoners. Once, dressed as a stylish gentleman out to ask for donations for the needy, he noticed two government agents staring at him suspiciously. Thinking quickly, Miguel spotted a Catholic lady he knew, and, going up to her, proceeded to put his arm around her waist, and walked right by the agents pretending to be the young lady's boyfriend. When sending letters, he would sign his code name, Cocol, taken from his favorite childhood treat. Through everything, Miguel was known for his faith, wit, humor, and joy.

Eventually, word got to the authorities of this bold young priest who was making them look stupid. The police began watching for Miguel. After a failed assassination attempt on the former president, Miguel was falsely accused, arrested, and sentenced to death. Hoping to make an example of him, the authorities held a public execution. When he was escorted onto the firing range, Miguel said a prayer, stood calmly, and refused a blindfold. He blessed the crowd and proclaimed his innocence. He then faced the men about to kill him, told them that he forgave them, and blessed them. With a rosary in one hand and a crucifix in the other, Miguel stretched out his arms like Jesus on the cross. He cried out in a strong voice, "¡*Viva Cristo Rey!*" ("Long live Christ the King!") Shots rang out and the 36-year-old Miguel bravely died.

The authorities had made sure to capture Miguel's death on camera, hoping to catch images of a pathetic priest pleading for mercy. They thought by killing him, they would scare people away from the Faith, so they published pictures of the execution in all the papers the next day. Instead, thirty thousand people lined the streets for his funeral. Word of Miguel's courageous martyrdom spread and inspired thousands to fight for their Catholic faith. Many of them carried with them the newspaper photos of Miguel's last moments. Today, after much conflict and many other martyrdoms, Catholics are free to worship in Mexico.

BLESSED

FULL NAME:
Miguel Pro

N NICKNAME:
Master of Disguise

Y YEARS: 1891–1927

C COUNTRY: Mexico

Miguel used his personality and talents to protect the Faith in Mexico. When you find yourself in need of courage or want some inspiration about how to use the gifts God gave you, talk to Miguel. He stands by your side now, asking you: "All this Christ did and suffered for us, and what are we doing for him?" Think about it!

2
ANTHONY

Hammer of Heretics

*He left a life of wealth and privilege, became
a humble, dishwashing Franciscan priest, and
ended up the Hammer of Heretics!*

Anthony of Padua was born in 1195 as Ferdinand Martins de Bul-hões in Lisbon, Portugal. At the age of fifteen, he decided to enter the priesthood and joined an Augustinian monastery. After moving to a remote monastery, Ferdinand focused on reading the Bible and studying the writings of the Church Fathers.

Eight years later, he watched as the bodies of five Franciscan missionaries were brought home to Portugal. The Franciscan Order, started by Francis of Assisi, who was still living at the time, encouraged their friars to live as Jesus did. Franciscan friars traveled simply and preached in the streets, telling people about the love of Christ. These five missionaries had been killed for preaching the Faith in Morocco. Ferdinand, inspired by their witness, decided that he, too, wanted to live the Gospel radically. He became a Franciscan, taking the name Anthony.

Anthony soon sailed for Morocco to start his preaching mission. On the way, he became very sick and had to stop in Portugal for treatment, a sudden storm blew his ship off course. Anthony ended up in Sicily and eventually made his way to mainland Italy.

ANTHONY SAID:
"Our thoughts ought by instinct to fly upwards from animals, men, and natural objects to their Creator. If created things are so utterly lovely, how gloriously beautiful must he be who made them! The wisdom of the worker is revealed in his handiwork."

Anthony was sent to a remote monastery to recover from his illness, and then went to the Franciscan provincial in northern Italy and asked to be instructed in the Franciscan way of life. Out of humility, Anthony never mentioned that he had studied theology for years.

One day, a group of Dominican friars came to visit for a retreat. They thought that the Franciscans would be giving the reflection, while the Franciscans thought that the Dominicans were supposed to be doing it. No one wanted to volunteer, so finally the Franciscan prior (the head of the monastery) drafted Anthony. Putting all his trust in the Holy Spirit to inspire him, Anthony began to preach. His dynamic way of talking, powerful, expressive voice, and total command of his subject shocked and impressed his audience. Anthony's brilliant theological mind could not remain hidden anymore. Saint Francis heard about Anthony and sent him to preach in northern Italy.

Anthony became known for his dynamic preaching. He evangelized all over Italy, France, and Spain. Never afraid of a confrontation, he enthusiastically defended and promoted the Faith to everyone, including heretics. (Heretics are people who claim to be part of the Church, but knowingly believe and teach things that are against what the Church, and Jesus, taught.) Because of the unflinching, bold way he debated, and his clear, forthright way of explaining the errors in his opponent's arguments, Anthony became known as the "Hammer of Heretics."

Anthony was also known for performing miracles. He was said to be able to bilocate (be in two places at one time). Once when Anthony was preaching, he suddenly remembered that he was supposed to be across town conducting a service. The people watched as he suddenly knelt down in prayer. Across town, the monks watched Anthony come forward and go through the service, then return to his room. At that same moment, Anthony got up and finished the service at the first church!

Another time, some heretics tried to poison Anthony at dinner. He simply made the Sign of the Cross over the food and proceeded to enjoy his meal with no problem at all. One time, when the heretics refused to listen to him, Anthony went over to the beach and began to preach. As the amazed people watched, fish of all sizes and shapes swam up to the edge of the water to hear Anthony's words. The people soon realized that if fish were gathering to listen to Anthony then they should listen too!

Anthony continued to preach and teach until his death. Because of his inspiring life and writings, he was declared a saint and a Doctor of the Church (a saint whose writings are especially influential and inspiring). Toward the end of his life, Anthony had a special book of the Psalms, in which he had written all his notes for his teaching. A novice who was leaving the order stole the book. Anthony prayed that he would get his book back, and the thief was moved to return it. Because of this, many people ask Anthony for help when something is lost. He has a reputation for being able to find anything from car keys, cell phones, and papers, to pets, people, jobs, and just about anything else you might have lost. He even has his own rhyme: "Tony, Tony, look around. Something's lost and must be found!"

So if you've lost something, need to make a speech, or you're looking for the right words to defend your faith, call on Anthony. He's there for you.

SAINT

FULL NAME:
Anthony of Padua

N NICKNAME:
Hammer of Heretics

Y YEARS: 1185–1231

C COUNTRY: Portugal

3
PIO

The Mystic

*He could bilocate and read people's souls, battled the devil,
and was given many incredible gifts to help people draw close
to God, yet he remained a humble, simple Franciscan.*

Padre Pio was born Francesco Forgione in Pietrelcina, Italy, in 1887. His parents were poor but very faithful Catholics. Francesco was only five when he decided he wanted to give his life to God! When he was fifteen, he joined the Capuchin Order. He was given the name of Pio and was ordained a priest in 1910. (Padre means "Father" in Italian.)

From an early age, Pio had received visions of Mary, Jesus, and his guardian angel. These continued after his ordination. He also had many battles with the Devil who knew that Pio's holiness and faith would save many souls. For this reason, the Devil tormented Pio, trying to shake his faith and scare him away from his mission. Pio fought back bravely. He knew the power of the name of Jesus and used it to drive the Devil away.

Pio was always thinking about God and praying. One of his favorite prayers was the Rosary, which he said was the best weapon against evil in the world. People began to notice his great faith and came to him for advice.

Pio knew confession was a powerful sacrament that helps us fight sin and get closer to

PIO SAID:
"Jesus is with you even when you don't feel his presence. He is never so close to you as he is during your spiritual battles. He is always there, close to you, encouraging you to fight your battle courageously. He is there to ward off the enemy's blows so that you may not be hurt."

SAINT

FULL NAME:
Padre Pio

N **NICKNAME:** The Mystic

Y **YEARS:** 1887–1968

C **COUNTRY:** Italy

God. He often said that confession was the soul's bath. During his lifetime, Pio heard over five million confessions! God always helped him in this ministry. One day, he was supposed to hear confessions, but a big crowd of people was blocking his way. A man suddenly saw Padre Pio walking over the people's heads toward the confessional. Suddenly, he disappeared and reappeared inside the confessional. The man thought he was dreaming, but when he made it to confession he asked Padre Pio how he had walked over the people. Padre Pio joking said, "I can assure you, my child, it's just like walking on the floor."

Pio received the gifts of healing, understanding languages, reading hearts and minds, and predicting future events. Pio never felt worthy of these God-given gifts, but knew he was to use them to help people believe and love God. One lady went into the confessional prepared to tell her sins, but she was so excited to be so close to the famous Pio that she forgot everything she was going to say. Pio asked her if she wanted him to talk for her. She agreed, and he proceeded to say everything that she had planned to tell him.

Many people looked to Pio for help and spiritual advice. Once, one of his spiritual children named Cecil was in a terrible car accident. His friend rushed to send a telegram to Padre Pio, to tell him about the accident and ask him to pray. But before he could send the telegram, the man at the telegraph office handed him a message from Padre Pio saying that he would pray for Cecil's recovery. After several months, Cecil and his friend traveled to see Pio. Curious, they asked Padre Pio how he had known about the accident, and how he had sent that telegram so quickly. Pio smiled and said, "Do you think angels go as slowly as the planes?"

During World War II, southern Italy fell into the hands of the Nazis. Pio had promised the people of San Giovanni Rotondo, where he lived, that the city would not be harmed. However, because it was now Nazi territory, a group of American bomber planes was ordered to bomb the city. As they arrived over the city, just as they were about to drop the bombs, a brown-robed friar appeared in the air in front of the planes! The airmen tried to drop the bombs, but the planes' mechanisms wouldn't release the weapons. The city was saved. Later, when the Nazis had been driven out, an American airbase was established close by. One of the airmen who had been on the bombing mission had a chance to visit the friary in San Giovanni Rotondo. He was shocked and amazed when he recognized the friar he had seen in the sky. It was Pio, who had never left the friary!

Pio also felt a great desire to help sinners and the souls in purgatory. God granted this desire and Pio received the stigmata. That means that the painful wounds of the crucifixion that Jesus received in his hands, feet, and side mysteriously appeared on Pio's body. Doctors carefully and thoroughly examined the wounds and determined that they were not normal. They did not heal even when treated, and they didn't become infected or smell bad. (In fact, witnesses said that the blood smelled like roses.) Pio joined the pain and suffering of his stigmata to those of Jesus on the cross to help sinners receive mercy and forgiveness. Pio suffered these wounds for over fifty years until they healed at his death at the age of eighty-one.

Through faith, prayer, and sacrifice, Pio lived an extraordinary life. Pio knew that all his amazing powers came from God, and were given to him for the good of others. He also knew that whatever happens in our lives, God is always with us. When you are worried about something, put it in God's hand and trust him. Like Pio said, "Pray, hope, and don't worry." Remember the power of the name of Jesus and wield the rosary. Wash your soul in confession as often as you can, and send your guardian angel to say hi to Pio!

4
CARLO

The Webmaster

The ultimate computer geek, teenaged Carlo used his
skills and the internet to introduce thousands to Jesus.

Carlo Acutis was born in London, England, in 1991. He and his family moved to Italy when he was just three months old.

Carlo prayed the Rosary every day, and whenever he passed a church, he stepped in to visit Jesus in the Blessed Sacrament. The Eucharist became a great source of inspiration and strength for him. Carlo would often wonder why there were long lines of people waiting for hours to see a concert or movie, yet no lines to see Jesus.

Carlo was well-liked in school and was known for helping kids who were having a rough time. Whenever any of his friends were struggling, Carlo would invite them to come home with him to talk out the problem and then get their minds off of it. When bullies were tormenting some of his classmates who had disabilities, Carlo stood up to the bullies and demanded that they stop. As a teenager, he volunteered to help children and the elderly. Just like any other kid, Carlo also liked hanging out and having fun with his buddies. He loved playing video games and soccer. Carlo had a weakness for sweets, which led to him putting on weight. Recognizing that he was overindulging and wanting to improve his self-control, Carlo kept a journal where he would write the good and bad he did that day. As he said, "What's the use of winning 1,000 battles if you can't beat your own passions?" This helped him learn to make the right choices and get closer to God.

> **CARLO SAID:**
> "Jesus is my great friend, and the Eucharist my highway to heaven."

27

Carlo was especially skilled with computers. In fact, he was a genius when it came to anything having to do with technology.

At the age of eleven, Carlo decided to use his computer skills to help people strengthen their faith. He wanted to create a website that would promote devotion to Jesus in the Eucharist. This website would list and describe Eucharistic miracles around the world, complete with pictures. He started to research and document the more than 136 Eucharistic miracles acknowledged by the Church. After several years, Carlo's project was complete: a virtual museum of Eucharistic miracles, with a website to showcase it. He also helped create panel presentations to be exhibited. Now, Carlo's website has been visited by thousands, and the exhibitions have been shown on five continents. His website is still online and available for viewing.

Carlo's time in front of the Blessed Sacrament brought him very close to Jesus. He would say, when "we face the sun we become tan … but when we place ourselves in front of the Eucharistic Jesus we become saints." His hours in front of Jesus gave him an inner strength, which he really needed when he was diagnosed with one of the worst types of leukemia (a type of blood cancer). His courage and faith never wavered. While going through extremely difficult treatments, he was asked if he was suffering too much pain. He replied that "there are people who suffer much more than me." He always offered up his suffering for "the Lord, the pope and the Church." Carlo died at the age of fifteen and is now on the path to sainthood.

You might ask why God let that happen. Why would God give cancer to an active, good guy like Carlo? The first thing we have to realize is that God didn't give him cancer. If we read the Book of Genesis in the Bible, we see that death came into the world because of the disruption and disharmony caused by sin. God did not create death. God loves us. He wants us to be happy. But by our disobedience and bad choices, we brought death and pain into the world. The one thing we know is that when bad things happen, God is right there beside us to give us strength and peace to help us through. God also always brings good out of evil. Look at Carlo. He was only fifteen when he died, yet now the story of his faith and devotion to the Eucharist will inspire people all over the world for many years to come. Those people who were inspired by Carlo will go out and be forces for good. Thousands will visit his website and see the exhibitions and will come to know Jesus. Most importantly, Carlo's witness will help those people to heaven, which is their ultimate happiness. His work goes on!

As Carlo said, "All people are born as originals, but many die as photocopies." To truly follow Jesus, you must be an original. You can't just follow the crowd and do what is popular. Don't give into peer pressure when everyone is doing something you know is wrong. Make the unpopular choice, if it is the right choice. You must do what is right and what you are called to do. You must be who God made you to be! If you find yourself going in the wrong direction and in need of some

BLESSED

FULL NAME:
Carlo Acutis

N NICKNAME:
The Webmaster

Y YEARS: 1991–2006

C COUNTRY: England, Italy

more self-control, try keeping a journal as Carlo did. Try to live so that the good list is much longer than the bad!

Carlo was an original. He took his talents and created a website that is still glorifying God and inspiring people around the world. Even though he only lived for fifteen years, he lived a life full of faith. He made a difference in the world. Carlo would be the first to tell you that, if you want to be inspired and changed, you should spend some time before the Blessed Sacrament, and receive Jesus in the holy Eucharist as often as possible. That was the source of Carlo's strength. Jesus is present and waiting for you. Spend some time before the Lord and see what happens. Carlo is right there with you!

5
BLACK ELK

The Medicine Man

This Native American warrior catechist created a bridge between his people and the Church while preserving and promoting his Lakota culture and traditions.

Black Elk was born in Powder River, Montana, in 1863. He was a member of the Oglala Lakota tribe (also called the Sioux). As a boy, he had a vision. He described the vision, saying, "I was standing on the highest mountain of them all, and round about beneath me was the whole hoop of the world. And while I stood there, I saw more than I can tell and, I understood more than I saw: for I was seeing in a sacred manner the shapes of all things in the spirit, and the shape of all shapes as they must live together like one being. And I saw that the sacred hoop of my people was one of many hoops that made one circle, wide as daylight and as starlight, and in the center few, one mighty flowing tree to shelter all the children of one mother and one father. And I saw that it was holy." (In Native American culture, the hoop represents the community in the circle of life.) Black Elk's vision told of how the earth and all people are connected under one creator. The elders of the tribe were amazed at his vision. Like his father and uncles, Black Elk grew up to be a medicine man and a warrior. (A Native American medicine man takes care of the physical and spiritual needs of his people.)

After gold was found in the Black Hills, which was sacred land to the Lakota people, pros-

> **BLACK ELK SAID:**
> "I send my people on the straight road that Christ's Church has taught us about. While I live, I will never fall from faith in Christ. I want to be a catechist the rest of my life."

SERVANT OF GOD

FULL NAME:
Nicholas Black Elk

N NICKNAME:
The Medicine Man

Y YEARS: 1866–1950

C COUNTRY: United States

pectors rushed to the area, breaking the treaties that had been made with the Native American people. The government demanded that the Lakota sell their sacred hills. Instead, the powerful Lakota nation fought back.

Twelve-year-old Black Elk followed his cousin Crazy Horse to fight against the U.S. Army. They joined the famous war chief Sitting Bull and helped defeat George Custer and his troops in the Battle of the Little Bighorn. In response, the government became determined to subdue the Lakota people any way they could. At the same time, there was a shortage of food for the Lakota because of the wasteful killing of the bison — the main source of food for the Lakota — by hired buffalo hunters. This forced the Lakota people to move onto government settlements called reservations.

Black Elk returned to working as a healer for his people on the reservation. He married his first wife, Katie War Bonnet, and they had three children. Katie became a Catholic, and they had their children baptized. After Katie died, Black Elk continued serving as a medicine man. One day, both he and a local Jesuit priest were called at the same time to minister to a dying boy. After talking with the priest that day, Black Elk accepted his invitation to study the Catholic Faith at the nearby Holy Rosary mission. After several weeks of intense study, Black Elk was baptized a Catholic and took the name of Nicholas. Two years after Katie's death, Black Elk married his second wife, Anna Brings White, a widow with two daughters. Anna was also a Catholic, and together they had three children. After Anna died in 1941, Black Elk moved in with his adult children and their families.

The Jesuit priests at the mission were impressed by Black Elk's enthusiasm and knowledge of the Scriptures and appointed him as a catechist. Life on the reservation was very difficult. Poverty and alcoholism were huge problems for the residents. As a catechist for his community, Black Elk not only taught his people about the love of Jesus, but he was also there for them in times of need to comfort and help them. He encouraged others to do the same. Black Elk was responsible for bringing hundreds of the Lakota people into the Church.

At a time when Native American traditions and customs were looked down upon by others, Black Elk would still proudly practice Lakota ways. He encouraged the people, especially the children, to remember and be proud of their traditions and culture. He tried to show them that the Lakota way and the Catholic Church together was a sacred path to salvation.

Right before he died, Black Elk predicted, "I have a feeling that when I die, some sign will be seen. Maybe God will show something … which will tell of his mercy." At his wake, the night sky was lit with an extremely beautiful display of the Aurora Borealis — the Northern Lights! Today, the highest mountain in the Black Hills has been renamed Black Elk Peak, and Black Elk has been named a Servant of God.

When Black Elk saw a vision of how the world could live in peace, love, and harmony, he did everything he could to help this dream become a reality. He brought hundreds of the Lakota people into the Church, where he had found the fulfillment and truth of his vision. And he helped bring the rich, beautiful spirituality of the Lakota into the Church. Today, Native American Catholics use some of their cultural traditions at Mass and in prayer.

Everyone has a history and heritage. The Church has recognized that it is richer when those different heritages are respected and welcomed. Black Elk knew that. He never stopped trying to change the world for the better. Let him inspire you to learn about other cultures and what they can offer.

6
JP2

The Skier

He was an actor, skier, poet, outdoorsman,
mystic, and a pope who is now a saint!

Before he became pope, John Paul II's name was Karol Wojtyła. Karol was born in Wadowice, Poland, in 1920. He and his family faithfully attended Mass at the church next door. Karol suffered many losses in his childhood. His mother died when he was eight and his brother died when Karol was twelve. Despite these sorrows, Karol found friends and comfort in sports and the outdoors. He was popular in school. He was a great soccer player and loved hiking, skiing, and kayaking, and also enjoyed writing and acting in plays.

When Karol was a young man, Poland was invaded, first by the Nazis and then by Communist Russia. The conquerors tried to destroy and suppress all Polish history, traditions, and religion. This only increased the Polish people's resolve to preserve their heritage. When Nazi Germany took over, the Nazi police closed the libraries, universities, and seminaries. Teachers and priests were killed. Polish people could be arrested or even shot for going to a play or concert, attending Mass, or even just speaking Polish instead of German.

After graduating at the top of his high school class, Karol went on to attend a university. A

> **JP2 SAID:**
> "Do not be afraid. Do not be satisfied with mediocrity. Put out into the deep and let down your nets for a catch. There is no place for selfishness and no place for fear! Do not be afraid, then, when love makes demands. Do not be afraid when love requires sacrifice."

year later, the university was shut down by the Nazis, but Karol, along with many other students and professors, continued to study in secret. All the while, Karol had to work long hours in a limestone quarry, and eventually in a chemical factory, in order to avoid deportation. Together with his university friends, Karol started an underground theater group that focused on Polish culture and used the Polish language to inspire their fellow Poles.

At this time, Karol was introduced to the teachings of St. John of the Cross, a Carmelite priest. Saint John taught Karol how to pray and work through difficult times, when you are suffering and God seems far away. Saint John said that by praying through dark times, you can become closer to God and grow spiritually. Karol took this teaching to heart. One day, the twenty-year-old Karol returned from work to find that his father had died. Karol prayed by his body all night. He felt so alone, and yet in his sorrow, he felt the presence of God. As Karol mourned his father, he also saw the suffering and persecution of the Jewish and Polish people under the Nazi regime. He turned to the only source of light he could find in that dark, twisted world — the Church. Even though Karol knew that his life would be in terrible danger, he felt God calling him to help his people, and became a priest. His seminary classes and ordination were all in secret.

As a young priest, Karol still loved spending time outdoors. He would take friends and young families on hikes and kayaking trips, and would celebrate Mass on the riverbank. Even though it was dangerous to be a priest in Communist Poland, Karol took that risk gladly in order to bring Jesus to his people. Becoming a priest didn't slow him down on the ski slopes either. He was known as the "Daredevil of the Tatras" for his skills in taking on the steepest slopes of Poland's Tatra Mountains.

This energetic priest was made bishop, then became cardinal of Kraków, Poland. In 1978, he was elected pope and took the name of Pope John Paul II. He became affectionately known as "JP2." As pope, JP2 took more trips than all the popes before him put together! He visited 129 countries on 104 international trips, traveling more than 700,000 miles. People all over the world were inspired by his deeply thoughtful writings. He fought for peace and freedom for everyone. At different stops in his travels, he would always enjoy being immersed in the people and culture. There are pictures of him wearing a hard hat, a feather headdress, getting dressed in a teepee, holding a koala, and swinging a hockey stick — to name just a few! But he didn't let being pope stop him from skiing. He would sit in the back seat of a friend's car, hiding his face behind a newspaper in order to sneak past all the security guards out of the Vatican. They would drive up into the mountains and find a deserted slope where JP2 would ski happily for the day.

JP2 had a great devotion to Our Lady. From the time he had lost his mother, JP2 had felt a special connection with the Blessed Mother. When he

SAINT

FULL NAME: Pope John Paul II

N **NICKNAME:** The Skier

Y **YEARS:** 1920–2005

C **COUNTRY:** Poland, Italy

was twenty, he had been introduced to the writings of St. Louis de Montfort about how wonderful it is to be consecrated to Mary. Later JP2 said, "I was already convinced that Mary leads us to Christ, but at that time I began to realize also that Christ leads us to his Mother." From that time on, JPII consecrated himself to Mary and took as his motto *Totus Tuus,* which in Latin means "All Yours." As pope, he promoted devotion to Mary and instituted the Luminous Mysteries of the Rosary.

In 1981, as JP2 rode standing in his popemobile blessing the crowd in Saint Peter's Square, a man tried to kill him. JP2 was shot several times and wounded badly. The bullets missed his main artery by millimeters and passed by the major organs. Everyone said it was a miracle. JP2 believed that Mother Mary had personally changed the path of the bullet so that he would live through the attack. He said, "Someone's hand had shot me, but Another Hand directed the bullet. For in everything that happened to me on that very day, I felt that extraordinary motherly protection and care, which turned out to be stronger than the deadly bullet." When he finally recovered, JP2 met with and forgave his attacker.

JP2 used his position as pope to help people all over the world. He spoke out for human rights and an end to abortion, urged acceptance and forgiveness, and encouraged respect for other cultures. He especially tried to get young people involved in changing the world for the better and created World Youth Day for them. World Youth Day is celebrated every two or three years, each time in a different country. Catholic young people gather to worship, get to know other young people from all over the world, and are inspired to return home and live the life of the Gospel. Perhaps one day you will be able to attend a World Youth Day!

JP2 never forgot his home country and used his political influence to help bring about the fall of communism in Poland and the fall of the Soviet Union. His many writings went around the world, inspiring people and causing them to think about life and their faith. During his final years, JP2 suffered from Parkinson's disease and other illnesses. Showing humble courage, patience, faith, and acceptance, he was a Christlike example for the world. He showed that we must value life, no matter what, until the very end. When he died at the age of eighty-four, more than four million people attended the funeral. It was the largest funeral in human history. Because of his great holiness and all he did for the Church, JP2 was canonized just nine years after his death.

Listen to the words of JP2 to the more than two million young people from 127 countries who attended World Youth Day 2000. He says those same words to you today: "It is Jesus who stirs in you the desire to do something great with your lives, the will to follow an ideal, the refusal to allow yourselves to be grounded down by mediocrity, the courage to commit yourselves, humbly and patiently to improving yourselves and society, making the world more human and more fraternal."

7
BRENDAN

The Navigator

He and a group of his monks set off across the
Atlantic in a leather boat to spread the Word of
God — maybe even as far as America!

Born in Tralee, Ireland, in 484, Brendan became a priest at the age of twenty-six. Brendan loved the passage of the Bible when Jesus says, "Go into the whole world and proclaim the Gospel to every creature" (Mk 16:15). He decided that this would be his mission. Being an expert sailor, Brendan traveled to Wales, Scotland, England, and France, building monasteries and churches wherever he went. Soon, he became the head of a community of more than three thousand monks! One day, a wandering monk told Brendan of his mysterious voyage to the Promised Land of the Saints. The monk said that he and a fellow hermit had sailed west and come upon a beautiful land. After hearing this story, Brendan decided that he should take the word of God to this new place. He and a group of his monks built a boat of woven sticks and tanned animal hides. They attached a mast and sail and set off across the Atlantic Ocean.

BRENDAN SAID:
"Help me to journey beyond the familiar and into the unknown.
"Give me the faith to leave old ways and break fresh ground with you.
"Christ of the mysteries, I trust you to be stronger than each storm within me. I will trust in the darkness and know that my times, even now, are in your hand. Tune my spirit to the music of heaven, and somehow, make my obedience count for you."

SAINT

FULL NAME:
Brendan of Clonfert

N NICKNAME:
The Navigator

Y YEARS: 484–577

C COUNTRY: Ireland

Brendan's voyage became immortalized in the legend *The Voyage of Saint Brendan the Abbot.* *The Voyage* tells of the many fascinating islands the monks came across, and the mysterious creatures they encountered — including a giant whale that they mistook for an island! While the tale uses very imaginative, descriptive language, scholars believe that a lot of it describes actual places and events. For instance, they discovered a place where "great demons threw down lumps of fiery slag from an island with rivers of gold fire" and "great crystal pillars" appeared — this could be describing the volcanic eruptions and icebergs around Iceland.

Brendan eventually sailed to a beautiful land of lush flowering plants and fruits. They found a guide who took them around the land, but they were halted by a great river. Soon afterward, the monks returned home. Brendan died shortly after telling of his adventures.

Today, some historians theorize that Brendan actually sailed all the way to America. Some of the sights and islands that Brendan described match sights and islands along the route from Ireland to America. Early Scandinavian writings talk of the Irish reaching America before the Vikings. A modern-day adventurer named Tim Severin even built a boat just like Brendan's and tried to sail it across the Atlantic to America, just to see if it was possible. He succeeded!

Brendan had no idea what he might run into out on the ocean, but he wanted to spread the good news of Jesus so much that he was willing to sail to the ends of the earth to do it. He knew there would be many unknown dangers, but he also knew that God was with him on his journey, so he wasn't afraid. Who knows what adventures God has in mind for you? Whatever your mission is, God is with you, and so is Brendan! Also, Brendan is the patron of travelers, so next time you are on a trip with your family, take the Navigator with you!

8
STANLEY

The Farmer

*A sports-loving, tractor-driving farm boy left
home to dedicate his life to people in need.*

Stanley Rother was born in 1935 in Okarche, Oklahoma, to a farming family. The oldest of three children, he was responsible for many chores, including feeding the chickens and gathering their eggs. Like many older brothers, he liked to play tricks. While gathering eggs with his little sister, he asked her to check under a hen again. His sister reached under the hen, and instead of an egg pulled out a big bull snake (they're not poisonous). Stanley started laughing hysterically and then ran as his sister screamed with fear and then with rage. She chased him out into the yard. Furious, she threw a can that hit him over the eye. It gave him a scar that he had the rest of his life, but he always insisted that it was worth it just to see her face when she pulled out that snake.

A small-town boy, Stanley grew up playing sports and helping out on the farm. He was also an altar boy at his church and went to Catholic school. He and his family prayed together every night. Although Stanley loved farming, he decided that he loved God more. He and his sister (the one from the snake story) both decided to enter religious life.

Stanley joined the seminary to study to become a priest. While there, he helped out with the gardening, did some plumbing and carpentry, and worked in the church, among other things. He did great — except for his

STANLEY SAID:
"God will take care of his own if we are in that group. Nothing will happen that isn't supposed to. It is all part of his great plan."

studies. Stanley had lots of trouble learning Latin and was asked to leave. Fortunately his bishop recognized the strength of his vocation, put in a good word for him, and transferred him to a different seminary. This time he succeeded! He made it through seminary and was ordained a priest.

After five years as a parish priest, Stanley volunteered to go to the Catholic Mission of Oklahoma in Guatemala. He was assigned to the small village of Santiago Atitlan. This village suffered terrible poverty and sickness. Children were dying from not enough good food. Many people had intestinal worms from polluted drinking water. Flu, diarrhea, and measles were common.

Stanley went to work. All his skills at farming and fixing things came in very handy as he worked hard to help his new people. He was once seen operating a bulldozer from seven in the morning to late in the afternoon. He stopped work only once a day, to say Mass. Along with digging new wells for clean water, he also started a farm to help grow healthy food for the community, a hospital clinic, and a school. He started the first Catholic radio station in the area to help teach even more villages about the love of Jesus. Even though in the past he had such trouble learning Latin, Stanley was able to learn Spanish quickly, and then learned how to speak Tz'utujil, the local Mayan language. He even translated the New Testament into Tz'utujil and said Mass in that language. The people grew to love their energetic young priest.

But things were not peaceful in the little town. There was a civil war going on in Guatemala. Since the Church was on the side of the poor people, those in power were coming after the priests. Several priests had already been murdered. After learning that his name was on a list of people the government wanted to kill, Stanley reluctantly went back home to Oklahoma. After a few months, he asked his bishop for permission to return to Santiago Atitlan. Father Stanley wrote an article for the Archdiocese of Oklahoma. In it he said: "This is one of the reasons I have for staying in the face of physical harm. The shepherd cannot run at the first sign of danger. Pray for us that we may be a sign of the love of Christ for our people, that our presence among them will fortify them to endure these sufferings in preparation for the kingdom."

Stanley went back to the people he cared so much about and celebrated Easter with them. A few months later, three assassins broke into the rectory at night when Stanley was sleeping. After a short struggle, they shot him. Stanley was officially declared a martyr by Pope Francis in 2016.

But that is not the end of Stanley's story. The devil may have thought he won when Stanley was killed, that people would forget about Stanley and his work would end. But God can always bring good out of anything. Stanley's story of faith and sacrifice continues to spread and inspire people across the world. He has been beatified and is on his way to sainthood. His work goes on in all those who are inspired by his story.

BLESSED

FULL NAME: Stanley Rother

NICKNAME: The Farmer

YEARS: 1935–1981

COUNTRY: United States, Guatemala

Stanley didn't let anything stop him. When he failed out of seminary, he tried again. When he saw the many needs of his people, he used all his talents and energy to help change their world for the better. He didn't even let the fear of death keep him from showing his people how much he cared. Sometimes fear keeps us from helping others or from speaking up against evil. Sometimes peer pressure talks us into doing something we know is wrong. Stanley knows how hard it is to face your fear and overcome it. Ask him to help you overcome your fears and difficulties, so you can go out and be a light in your world!

And the next time you have a big game you're nervous about, or a test in a subject you're having trouble with, ask Stanley to say a prayer for you. He knows how it is!

9
JUSTUS TAKAYAMA

The Samurai

A samurai warrior who gave everything for Christ!

Takayama Justus Ukon was born in 1552 in Haibara, Japan. His father was the lord of Sawa Castle and owned a lot of property. He also had control over a large army. In 1549, his shogun appointed him to judge a Jesuit missionary, Father Videla. After listening and talking with the missionary, Takayama's father decided to become a Christian. He and the whole family, including Takayama who was twelve at the time, were baptized.

Takayama was given the name of Justus. As the eldest son, Takayama would inherit his father's castle and authority. In preparation, he was trained to become a samurai warrior. Like his father, he practiced *bushido* — the life of the sword, which meant that he must value loyalty, courage, truth, compassion, and honor above everything else. As a samurai, Takayama fought in many wars and conflicts and become known for his courage. At the age of twenty-one, Takayama's father retired and Takayama became *daimyō*. Two years later, Takayama married a Christian woman named Giusta Kuroda and they had three sons (two of whom died as babies) and a daughter together.

During Takayama's life, there was a lot of fighting in Japan. The warlords were in a constant conflict with each other. Sawa Castle was lost and Takayama and his family had to flee. They found protection under another war-

POPE FRANCIS SAID ABOUT TAKAYAMA:
"He remained faithful to Christ and to the Gospel; for this, he is a wonderful example of strength in the Faith and dedication in charity."

BLESSED

FULL NAME:
Justus Takayama

 **NICKNAME:** The Samurai

 **YEARS:** 1552–1615

 **COUNTRY:** Japan

lord, Oda Nobunaga. Takayama eventually fought his way to owning another castle, with lands and armies.

Because Takayama now had power and wealth, he was able to help the Jesuit missionaries spread the story of Jesus throughout Japan. Takayama would often use the traditional Japanese tea ceremony to evangelize. He would use the solemn symbolic ceremony to strengthen friendships, and then take the opportunity to talk about Jesus and the Gospel with the other nobles. He built churches and seminaries. It is said that 18,000 of the 25,000 people in his land became Catholic because of Takayama's support and help. This lasted until Nobunaga was killed. Life changed for Takayama when Nobunaga died and was succeeded by his grandson Hideyoshi.

At first, Hideyoshi was impressed with Takayama's bravery and samurai skills, and treated him with great respect and honor. However, he didn't like Takayama's Christianity and his support of the foreign missionaries. Soon, Hideyoshi decided that he didn't like Christianity at all, and that it was a threat to Japan. He ordered all Christians to give up their faith and began persecuting them, even crucifying some believers.

While many did give up their faith, Takayama refused. His friends tried to talk him into giving up Catholicism, but he wouldn't betray Christ. Hideyoshi wanted to crucify Takayama also, but was talked out of it by his advisors. They knew Takayama was greatly respected and famous through-out Japan for his courage in battle, support of Japanese culture including the tea ceremony, poetry, and architecture, as well as his well-known faith-ful love of his wife, Giusta. Hideyoshi gave him a choice: give up Christi-anity or lose everything. Takayama chose Christ! Hideyoshi took away all of his lands, armies, and money. Takayama and his family lived as exiles in their own land for several decades. Word spread of what he had done. The Jesuit priests he had protected and helped wrote books about their time in Japan with Takayama and about his life of good works and sacrifice. He even received a letter from Pope Sixtus V that encouraged him to stand fast in the Faith.

Hideyoshi then declared that Christianity was against the law. All missionaries and Christians were given the choice to give up their faith, leave Japan, or die. The shogun thought that Takayama might gather his allies and fight, but instead the samurai left peacefully with his wife Giusta, his married daughter, Lucia Yokoyama, and his five grandsons. Takayama also brought with him a group of around 350 Christians and missionaries. They sailed to the Philippines, where the Jesuit missionaries had brought word of Takayama, the great Christian military hero. They welcomed him as the samurai who protected priests and Christians, built hospitals and schools, brought many to the Faith, and gave up everything for Jesus. Un-fortunately, the long years of hardship in Japan and the difficult trip were too much for him. Takayama died forty-four days later. He was given a Catholic funeral with the highest military honors. When Takayama was beatified, Pope Francis said about him that "Rather than compromise, he renounced honors and prosperity and accepted humiliation and exile."

Takayama was dedicated to his life as a samurai warrior. He lived *bushido* — a life of loyalty, courage, truth, compassion, and honor. When he had to choose between his earthly ruler and his heavenly Lord, he knew what his choice must be. Even though it cost him everything, Takayama knew he had to stay true to his faith.

Takayama is known as Christ's samurai. Can you be Christ's samurai too? Can you live a life of loyalty, courage, truth, compassion, and hon-or? Can you stand up for your Catholic faith when challenged? Look to Takayama for inspiration and help!

10
WALTER

The Tenacious

He was trouble from the beginning, but his stubbornness helped him survive a horrific prison camp and become a force for good!

Born in Shenandoah, Pennsylvania, in 1904, Walter Ciszek was the seventh of thirteen children. Walter grew up to be a bully, had no use for school, and loved to fight. He became the leader of a street gang and was in trouble all the time. Not knowing how to stop Walter's bad behavior, his father took him to the local police station and asked them to send him to reform school. The police refused, and Walter continued his wild ways until the eighth grade. It was then that Walter shocked his parents and everyone who knew him when he informed them that he had decided to be a priest! No one believed he was serious until Walter left for the seminary. He decided to become a Jesuit because he thought the training would be a challenge. Once there, he was determined to prove how tough he really was. He got up early to run five miles and swam regularly in ice-cold lakes. One Lent, he ate only bread and water for forty days — just to prove he could. When others worried that he might get sick or hurt himself, Walter only laughed.

While training as a priest, Walter learned of the desperate situation of the Russian Catholics persecuted under the Communist Soviet Union. Priests and religious were either killed or im-

WALTER SAID:
"God has a special purpose, a special love, a special providence to all those he has created. Every moment of our life has a purpose, that every action of ours, no matter how dull or routine or trivial it may seem in itself, has a dignity and a worth beyond human understanding."

prisoned, and there were very few remaining to minister to the people. Walter decided that this was where God wanted him. His superiors agreed to let him go, on the condition that he finish his studies first. Walter studied at the Russian college in Rome and was ordained a priest.

Because the Soviet Union refused to let any priests enter Russia, Walter was sent first to Poland. Walter and another priest devised a way to sneak into Russia as refugees. Walter pretended to be a Russian lumber worker and managed to work undercover in a lumber camp. He spent several months hauling and stacking heavy logs with the other workers. Then his cover was blown, and he was arrested. Knowing he was a priest and thinking that he was spying for Germany, the Soviet police threw Walter into prison. After he was tortured, medically drugged, mentally manipulated, and threatened with death, he signed papers saying that he was guilty.

Walter describes this moment as the darkest moment of his life, yet it was through this darkest moment that he had his deepest conversion. He realized that even though he had always prayed and asked for God's help, he never really thought that he needed it. He had always thought that he could handle anything and everything himself. Now, he decided to give himself over totally to God's will, whatever that might be. This new conversion of heart gave Walter a renewed faith and energy. Because of his "confession of guilt," Walter was sentenced to fifteen years of hard labor in the Siberian Gulag. It was there that Walter finally began his mission.

The conditions in the gulag were horrible. People were starving. They were cruelly overworked, and their clothing and housing were not at all warm enough for the bitterly cold weather. The prison officials didn't even hand out winter clothes until October when the temperature was already thirty degrees below zero! Walter secretly said Mass and distributed holy Communion, baptized, heard confessions, helped the sick and dying, and tried to bring hope and faith to his fellow prisoners. When the guards found out what he was doing, they punished him by giving him the hardest jobs. He had to crawl through hazardous mines, shovel coal for fifteen hours straight, and dig sewer trenches — all in below-zero weather. Finally, fifteen long years passed, and Walter was released. He was not allowed to leave Russia, but he could write to his sister in America.

Once released, Walter got to work. People were so grateful to find a priest that they came from miles around. Walter spent hours before and after busy with baptisms, marriages, and confessions. That was when he was called into the secret police office. His passport was canceled, and he was given forty-eight hours to leave town! Walter moved to another town and in a couple of months had a thriving parish of 800 people. He continued to enthusiastically minister to the grateful people, despite constant harassment from the officials. Then the police notified Walter to be ready to leave in three days. Walter was sure that he was going to be arrested again. Instead, he was told that his permission to leave Russia had been arranged. He had been exchanged for two Russian spies caught in America. He was going home!

SERVANT OF GOD

FULL NAME:
Walter Ciszek

N **NICKNAME:**
The Tenacious

Y **YEARS:** 1904–1984

C **COUNTRY:** United States, Russia

Walter returned to America, where he spent the rest of his life writing books, teaching, and counseling. He was often asked why he had escaped death when so many others in Russia had died of beatings, illness, firing squad, starvation, and freezing. His answer was always the same: God wanted him to live to tell his story so that others could understand that God has a special purpose for each of us and that every moment has dignity and worth. He continued spreading this message until his death in 1984.

Those physical challenges Walter put himself through during his younger years helped build up his body to survive one of the most terrible prisons ever. He wanted to beat every challenge, but he came to realize that only by accepting whatever God wanted for him could he truly conquer all. He realized that God has a special purpose for each of us. He wanted everyone to realize that, by living in God's will, everything you do is important. Ask Walter to help you set your ego aside and put your life in God's hands. The world encourages pride and selfishness. Everyone wants to be famous, first, and best. But power doesn't come from the outside; true power comes from within when God is in your heart and soul. Only when Walter let his ego go, realized that he couldn't do everything by himself, and gave himself over to God's will, could God give him his mission and the strength and inspiration to complete it.

There is a mission in this life that God has set aside for only you to do. It may be something dramatic or it may be to just live your life the best you can, showing God's love to others. Walter dedicated his life to trying to get people to realize that. He's waiting to help you find your mission and dedicate your life to God. He wants to inspire you to have that same determination he had! He wants you to have the humility to hand your life over to God in all things. Let God take over and watch what happens!

11
MARTIN

Miracle Man

Discriminated against from birth, he became a wonderworker who was loved by both people and animals!

In 1579, Martin de Porres was born in Lima, Peru. He was the son of a freed slave woman from Panama of African and native descent and a Spanish nobleman. His father abandoned the family when Martin was very young. At that time in Peru, anyone with African blood was greatly discriminated against and treated badly. As a mixed-race child, Martin, his mother, and his younger sister struggled to survive. Eventually, Martin's father stepped up and decided to support and educate his children. He sent Martin to barber school. In those days, barbers not only cut hair, but they were also surgeons. Martin learned how to set bones, dress wounds, perform surgeries, treat diseases, and make medicines from herbs.

Martin had always been drawn to the Church and loved helping the poor. At the age of fifteen, Martin decided to enter the Dominican Order. Peruvian law of that time made it against the law for anyone of African or native South American descent to become full members of a religious order. After Martin had been with the Dominicans for eight years, his superior turned a blind eye to the law and allowed Martin to take vows as a lay Dominican brother. Even though he was only a third-order Dominican, Martin was granted permission to wear the habit and worked in

> **MARTIN SAID:**
> "Everything, even sweeping, scraping vegetables, weeding a garden, and waiting on the sick, could be a prayer if it were offered to God."

SAINT

FULL NAME:
Martin de Porres

N NICKNAME: Miracle Man

Y YEARS: 1579–1639

C COUNTRY: Peru

the infirmary, as well as doing farming, laundry, and kitchen tasks. Soon, sick people from all walks of life were coming to Martin for care, and he became known for miraculous cures. Martin treated slaves and noblemen alike: with kindness. He also opened a children's hospital and orphanage to help the poor children living in the slums of Lima.

Even though he still encountered ridicule and prejudice, Martin kept his gentle humor and dignity. To him, nothing mattered more than caring for the poor. Once he found a beggar lying on the side of the road, covered with sores. Martin gently picked him up, carried him to the monastery, and gently laid the beggar in his own bed. When one of the other friars disapproved, Martin told him: "Compassion, my dear brother, is preferable to cleanliness. Reflect that with a little soap I can easily clean my bed covers, but even with a torrent of tears I would never wash from my soul the stain that my harshness toward the unfortunate would create."

Martin continued to pray constantly. The other monks would often see a bright unearthly light coming from Martin's room when he was immersed in prayer. He was even seen to levitate while in deep prayer before the Blessed Sacrament. Once, he was praying with such fervor that the step he was kneeling on actually caught fire. Despite the noise and chaos that followed, Martin remained in such deep prayer that he didn't even notice! He received the supernatural gifts of predicting events before they happened, and knowing information without being told.

Martin's mission was helping people, and he didn't let little things like locks or distance keep him from those in need. During an epidemic, a group of sick monks were locked away in a section of the convent to keep them isolated from the other monks. Miraculously, Martin repeatedly passed through the door (which remained locked) to treat the sick monks. Martin was also able to bilocate. There were reports of Martin ministering to people in Algeria, China, France, Japan, Mexico, and the Philippines, although he never left Lima, Peru.

Martin was also known for his love of animals and his ability to communicate with them. When two new bulls that had just been brought to the monastery began fighting continually, Martin went out and gently asked them to get along. There were no more problems with the bulls. Another time, the monastery became overrun with mice. They were chewing on everything and getting into the food. The monks wanted to poison them, but Martin had another idea. He went through the monastery, asking the mice to meet him out in the garden. Hundreds of mice followed him into the garden where Martin told them that if they stayed outside, he would bring them food and care for them. The mice obeyed him. Martin even set up an animal shelter at his sister's house, where he treated sick animals.

By the time Martin died at the age of sixty, he was already considered a saint by everyone who knew him. He was officially canonized in 1962.

Sometimes hurts and wrongs that have been done to us can seem to be all-consuming. We focus on the negative and it makes our life miserable. Martin had a hard beginning. But with love and humor, he directed his gifts toward helping those in need, both human and animals. Don't let past or even present wrongs define who you are. Don't let evil win. Instead, like Martin, focus on giving. Help your family, neighbors, and pets, wherever you see a need. Martin showed God's love and care to everyone, even the smallest of creatures. Be like Martin, considerate and charitable to all!

12
GUIDO

The Surfer

Being at the beach, friends, and surfing — Guido loved nothing more than these three things ... until he discovered God.

Born in Rio de Janeiro, Brazil, in 1974, Guido Schäffer grew up hanging with his friends at the beach. He loved playing sports, but most of all, he loved surfing. He spent hours riding the waves. He also attended church regularly and went to a prayer group started by his mother. Faithful Catholics, Guido's family prayed together every night. He would often reach out to friends and invite them to come to church or prayer group.

Guido loved to help people, so when he got older, he decided to become a doctor like his father. While in medical school, he started his own prayer group for the youth of his parish. Guido was a dynamic speaker and was very good at counseling and inspiring his patients, coworkers, and the youth of his prayer group. As a doctor, Guido often took care of patients the other doctors didn't want to treat, such as those with HIV. He tried to treat the whole person, not just the illness. He would often talk about Jesus and his faith while treating his patients. Patients began asking for him because of his wonderful bedside manner.

GUIDO SAID:
"Love is to live this life intensely with eyes fixed on Jesus. Love is to search for God in all moments of our existence. Love is to think of God, dream of God, speak of God, desire death to be face to face with the Lord. One who loves gives himself, dedicates himself, and searches in everything in the desire of the Loved One. All our actions should show the love of God."

Despite his busy schedule, Guido still made time for surfing, which he said was the best place to find God. He prayed each time before entering the water, often inviting other beach-goers to join in prayer right there on the beach. In the beauty of God's ocean, he could feel God and would talk to him. Guido loved the water so much that he once told some friends that he hoped God would allow him to die in the sea, where he could feel God's presence so strongly.

Guido had a girlfriend and was planning on getting married until he went on a retreat. There he heard a priest speak on the Bible passage Tobit 4:7, which says: "Give alms from your possessions to all who live uprightly, and do not let your eye begrudge the gift when you make it. Do not turn your face away from any poor man, and the face of God will not be turned away from you." Guido felt called by God and prayed, "Jesus, help me care for the poor." The next week, he met some Missionaries of Charity (sisters from the order started by Mother Teresa) who spend their lives helping the poor. Guido realized that here was the answer to his prayer. He began working with the Missionaries, using his medical skills to help the homeless. He persuaded several of the doctors he worked with to help too. He spoke to his prayer group to inspire them, and they began collecting donations and going out into the streets to help. While he did all this, he would always take the chance to talk about Jesus with his patients and pray with them. One of the doctors working with Guido recommended that he read a book about St. Francis of Assisi. After reading the book, Guido decided to become a priest. This amazed and surprised his family — and of course, his girlfriend!

Guido entered the seminary while continuing to volunteer as a doctor to those in need. He always had time for everyone and treated them, no matter who they were, with respect and kindness. He also used his speaking talents and warm personality to spread the good news of Jesus on the local Catholic radio station. Guido's energy, enthusiasm, and caring smile made him friends wherever he went.

Through everything, he always tried to fit in a little time for surfing, where he felt so close to God. On one of his days off, Guido went to the beach with a friend. The waves were high, but nothing he hadn't surfed before. He and his friend said a prayer together before going in.

Guido paddled out. A large wave rolled in. Guido tried to dive his board underneath, but the board struck his head, knocking him unconscious. His friend dragged him to shore, but it was too late. Guido, the surfing seminarian, had died just as he had hoped he would: in the glory of God's ocean.

After his death, word spread of this energetic young man of faith who had dedicated his life to helping the poor. People began referring to him as the Surfer Angel. They started praying to him to ask God to help them with their problems and illnesses. Many cures have been reported! Guido's sister tells of the time a lifeguard was drowning. He

SERVANT OF GOD

FULL NAME: Guido Schäffer

NICKNAME: The Surfer
YEARS: 1974–2009
COUNTRY: Brazil

saw a bright light. Then he saw and felt two young men drag him out. Afterward, he discovered that he was rescued by only one man. He was even more surprised when he saw a picture of Guido and recognized him as the other man who pulled him out.

Next time you visit the ocean, take a walk in the woods, or look up at the night sky glittering with stars, take some time to really appreciate the glory of God's creation. Feel the spray of the sparkling waves that crash onto the shore. Feel the soft breeze and the warm sun. Hear the sound of life all around you. Listen to God. Guido heard God asking him to help the poor and sick. He answered that call with an enthusiastic yes! He is still helping people today. Listen … what is God asking you to do?

13
ALBERT

The Scientist

*Referred to as the teacher of all there is to know, he was
a consummate scientist, theologian, and philosopher,
and became known as Albert the Great!*

Albert was born around 1200 in Lauingen, Germany, to a family of knights. Albert loved to learn, and as a young man attended the University of Padua. While studying, he heard a Dominican priest preaching and decided to join that order. He became a Dominican priest. He continued his studies and then started to teach at different universities, eventually ending up at the University of Paris. Among his students was a quiet young man who was his prized pupil. This student would go on to become one of the greatest philosophers and theologians in history: St. Thomas Aquinas.

Albert was an expert in many of the sciences such as logic, psychology, biology, meteorology, mineralogy, zoology, astronomy, and chemistry. He especially loved philosophy and introduced the scientific principles of Aristotle into regular Dominican studies.

He was a scientist, and, at the same time, a devout man of faith. Along with his studies and experiments, he loved his duties as a priest. He was appointed bishop of Regensburg and ordered to put an end to the many abuses that were happening there. He founded the oldest German university, the University of Cologne, and counseled kings. He continued teaching,

ALBERT SAID:
"The greater and more persistent your confidence in God, the more abundantly you will receive all that you ask."

SAINT

FULL NAME:
Albert the Great

N NICKNAME: The Scientist

Y YEARS: 1200–1280

C COUNTRY: Germany

experimenting, and writing until he died in his eighties, leaving behind forty-one volumes full of careful, exact, scientific, philosophical, and theological documents.

In today's world, some people say that you cannot be both a person of science and a person of faith. Albert would strongly disagree! He loved science and learning, yet it did not conflict with his faith in God at all. Albert knew that all of God's creation tells us about its creator. His faith helped him appreciate the marvelous works of God through the natural world.

The Catholic Church has always encouraged science and scientific discovery. Catholic missionaries were the ones who brought the scientific method to Asia and contributed to the development of pendulum clocks, barometers, telescopes, and microscopes. Catholic astronomers were the first to note colored bands on Jupiter, rings around Saturn, and the connection between the moon and tides. The Church maintains and operates an observatory where researchers contribute to our knowledge of astronomy, cosmology, and physics. The big bang theory was conceived and developed by Father Georges Lemaitre, a priest, professor, and member of the Pontifical Academy of Science. The Pontifical Academy of Science was founded by Pope Pius XI in 1936. Still very active today, the Pontifical Academy of Science is an academy where the greatest scientific minds of our time come together from all over the world to meet in the Vatican to discuss and encourage research in the mathematical, physical, and natural sciences.

By observing, categorizing, and describing the world and things around him, Albert blazed the way for future researchers to build upon the ideas and theories in his writings. He encouraged rational thinking, saying that "all that is truly rational is compatible with the Faith revealed in Sacred Scriptures." He gave God the credit for all his discoveries and findings, saying, "Every science and knowledge proceeds from God. … This science cannot be separated from the One who has communicated it unto me." Albert knew that science helps us to see and appreciate the marvelous designs of God. He said, "In studying nature we have not to inquire how God the Creator may, as he freely wills, use his creatures to work miracles and thereby show forth his power; we have rather to inquire what Nature with its immanent causes can naturally bring to pass." Learning how God works through nature helps us discover the very truth of God.

Pope Benedict XVI said, "How many scientists, in fact, in the wake of Saint Albert the Great, have carried on their research inspired by wonder at and gratitude for a world which, to their eyes as scholars and believers, appeared and appears as the good work of a wise and loving Creator!"

Albert knew that the more we find out about our world, the more we know about God and his ways. He said, "The whole world is theology for us because the heavens proclaim the glory of God!" Albert, the patron saint of scientists, knew that science and faith go hand in hand in the search for truth — that is to say, in search of God. So next time you hear people say that you can't believe in both God and science, set them straight! Make Albert proud!

14
FRANCIS

The Animal Whisperer

*Originally just out for a good time, he gave everything up
to live like Jesus, spread his word, and love his creatures!*

Francis of Assisi was born in 1182 in Assisi, Italy, to a rich merchant family. Francis was baptized Catholic, but grew up spoiled and did whatever he wanted — usually drinking and partying with his many friends. Then he decided that he wanted the glory and excitement of being a knight. When his town of Assisi declared war on the next town, Francis got his chance.

Unfortunately, Assisi lost the fight, and Francis was captured. He spent the next year chained in a dark, damp dungeon waiting for his father to pay his ransom. Once the ransom was paid and he was released, Francis went back to partying!

Then Francis tried again to ride off to war to become a knight. On the way, he had a dream in which God told him that he was going the wrong way, so he turned around and went home. Soon after, he was out riding and met a leper (a person with a disease where you get covered with sores). Because of the disease, the leper looked horrible and smelled worse. Francis, who loved beauty and was very picky, suddenly got the urge to give the

FRANCIS SAID:
"All who love the Lord with their whole heart, their whole soul and mind, and with their strength, and love their neighbor as themselves, and who despise the tendency in their humanity to sin, receive the Body and Blood of Our Lord, Jesus Christ, and bring forth from within themselves fruits worthy of true penance."

leper a kiss of peace. He got down off his horse, took the leper's filthy hand in his, and kissed it. The leper returned the kiss. After he got back on his horse, Francis turned to give the leper a wave. The road was empty! Francis felt a rush of joy. He felt he had passed a test from God.

Later, he went to the little, tumbledown church of San Damiano in Assisi. In prayer, Francis heard Christ on the cross tell him, "Francis, go and rebuild my church which, as you see, is falling down." Looking around, Francis decided that Jesus wanted him to repair the crumbling church building. He ran to his father's shop, took some valuable cloth, and sold it to get the money to repair the church. Francis's father was furious. He dragged Francis to court in front of the bishop and the whole town. He demanded the money back and said that he didn't want Francis as his son anymore. The bishop told Francis to return the money, and that God would provide for his needs. When Francis heard this, he returned the money. Then he took off all his fancy clothes and handed them back to his father, ready to start a new life imitating Christ. Wearing only rags, he went off singing.

Francis became a beggar, going from house to house asking for materials to rebuild the church of San Damiano. He worked hard until the church was repaired. Eventually, it occurred to Francis that God was calling him not just to rebuild San Damiano, but to rebuild the Catholic Church. Francis decided that he would follow in the steps of Jesus for the rest of his life and live in poverty as Jesus had. Francis put on a rough, brown robe and tied a rope around his middle. He owned nothing, slept wherever he could, and begged for scraps of food to eat. Then he began to preach about Jesus and the Church. He had a true love for the holy Eucharist, and great respect for the priests who could give him this wonderful sacrament. Other men saw his joy and the Christlike way he lived, and they wanted to join him and live the same way. Soon Francis had a group of followers. He gave those who wanted to follow him a simple rule: follow the teachings of Our Lord Jesus Christ and walk in his footsteps.

Francis also started an order for women headed by St. Clare of Assisi (today they are known as the Poor Clares). He also formed the Third Order, which was for laypeople who couldn't become nuns or friars. Today there are thousands of Franciscans all over the world doing God's work!

Francis felt that everything God created was his family. He was known for his love of animals and referred to them as his brothers and sisters. Once, a wolf was terrorizing the town of Gubbio, killing people and sheep. The people asked Francis to come and help. Francis went out to where the wolf had been seen. The wolf charged out of the woods, growled, and bared his teeth. Just as he was about to attack, Francis made the Sign of the Cross over the wolf. The wolf laid down at Francis's feet. From then on, the wolf became a pet of the town.

Because of his great love and closeness to Jesus, the Lord gave him a special gift. Two years before his death, Francis was praying to share in Jesus' passion when he received the stigmata, which are the wounds

SAINT

FULL NAME: Francis of Assisi

NICKNAME: The Animal Whisperer

YEARS: 1182–1226

COUNTRY: Italy

of Christ, in his hands, feet, and side. Despite the pain caused by the wounds, Francis was overcome with joy to share in the suffering of Jesus. Francis died singing, joyful to the end! He was declared a saint in 1228.

As a young man, Francis thought he could find happiness in partying. Then he thought he would find happiness by being a knight. It was only when he gave everything up for Jesus that he was truly free and happy. Where are you looking for happiness? The world around you will tell you that happiness is in having lots of money and the latest gadgets, but Francis found true happiness living the Gospel, and in the True Presence of Jesus in the holy Eucharist. He wants you to know the freedom and joy he experienced. Ask him to help you find it.

15
JOSEPH

The Flying Friar

He was sickly, a bad student, and had a nasty temper,
but God helped him change into a caring priest
who helped the poor, healed people, and flew!

Joseph of Cupertino was born in Cupertino, Italy in 1603. His father died a few months before Joseph was born. Unfortunately, Joseph's father had owed a lot of money, so the people who he owed took his house and possessions to pay the bills. Joseph was born in a shed behind the house where his mother was hiding from the bill collectors.

Joseph never had enough to eat and was often sick. He had a lot of trouble learning to read and write and never learned to read or write well. He was forgetful and clumsy and his mother often lost patience with him. She would yell at him and hit him. Because of this, Joseph developed a bad temper and a really bad self-image. For the rest of his life, he would refer to himself as "dumb as an ass."

When a Franciscan friar came to town, he impressed Joseph so much that Joseph decided to become a priest. But because of his lack of education, Joseph had trouble finding an order to accept him. After much searching, he found a Franciscan community that offered to take him on trial as a lay brother. Unfortunately, the trial did not go well. It seems that Joseph couldn't do anything right. He was always dropping dishes and forgetting what he was supposed to do. He

JOSEPH SAID:
"My kind protector, studying is often hard for me, harsh and tiring. You can make it easy and pleasant."

SAINT

FULL NAME:
Joseph of Cupertino

Ⓝ **NICKNAME:** The Flying Friar

Ⓨ **YEARS:** 1603–1663

Ⓒ **COUNTRY:** Italy

couldn't follow the simplest directions or do the easiest task. Finally, the community decided that he had to turn in his habit and leave. Joseph said that was the hardest day of his life.

Joseph did not lose hope. Through his constant prayers, he managed to find work as a servant in a Franciscan friary. Joseph was made the keeper of the friary mule. Joseph was determined to make the best of his second chance. He began to pray more and do penance and fast, often eating only on Thursdays and Sundays. He became more gentle and careful. He went out begging for the poor. He was allowed to enter the Franciscan Order and studied to be a priest. He prayed that God would help him pass his studies. At his final examination, to his relief, Joseph was only asked the few questions he actually knew the answer to. Joseph passed!

Then Joseph started levitating. While he was praying or saying Mass, he would rise several feet in the air. During Christmas Mass, while carols were being sung, he flew up and knelt in the air above the altar! Another time, he flew into a tree while out begging for the poor. Occasionally, he would rise up in the dining room while holding plates of food. Once some workmen were struggling to get a large cross on the top of a church. Joseph took the cross and floated up to the roof of the church to put it in place. The most famous levitation came when he met with the pope. Joseph bent down to kiss the pope's feet and both he and the pope began to rise. Joseph was seen to fly more than seventy times, and sometimes would be up in the air for more than seven hours. His levitations were seen sometimes by large crowds and were also testified to by other priests, doctors, and princes.

Because of his faith and holiness, God gave Joseph other gifts that could be called superpowers. Joseph used these gifts to help people believe in and draw closer to God. He could heal people simply by touching them. Once, he made a blind child see. He could read minds and would often surprise fellow friars by knowing what they were going to say before they said it. He made several predictions that came true. As Joseph did these amazing things and gave God glory, people were inspired and came to believe in the Lord. He was also said to be able to talk to animals and they would listen! Once, he sent a sparrow to a convent to help the nun's singing. After one of the sisters shooed away the sparrow by mistake, the sparrow didn't return. The sisters told Joseph what had happened. He informed the sisters that the sparrow hadn't come to be insulted, but that he would apologize to the sparrow for the shooing. The sparrow returned.

As word of this flying holy man spread, more and more people came to see him. People loved going to confession to him. His compassionate words and advice changed many lives and increased the Faith of all who spoke to him. At the age of sixty, Joseph got sick and predicted that Jesus would be coming to get him soon. He died soon afterward.

Joseph had a rough childhood. He had disabilities and a bad temper. But God had created Joseph for a purpose. Through his faith in God, Joseph rose above his personal problems (literally) to reach out to those in need. He found happiness and contentment just spending time with God. God has a purpose for you too. Spend some time with Jesus. Like Joseph, you never know how high God will take you! And don't forget, if you are having difficulties in school or have a big test coming up, remember that Joseph had the same problem. He's been there. Ask him to help!

16
AUGUSTUS

The Trailblazer

*He faced down prejudice and broke barriers to
become the first Black priest in America!*

Augustus Tolton was born a slave in 1854 in Ralls County, Missouri. When the Civil War started, Augustus's father escaped to join the Union Army and fight for his family's freedom. After he left, Augustus's mom decided that the rest of the family should also try to escape. Augustus was only nine years old. One night, Augustus, his mom, his brothers, and his sister slipped away. They headed quickly through the woods to the Mississippi riverbank. If they could cross the river into Illinois, they would be free. They got into a rowboat and started to row frantically. Confederate soldiers spotted the escaping slaves and started firing their guns at them. Finally, Augustus and his family reached the Illinois shore. They were safe! They all knelt and thanked God for their freedom.

Augustus and his family settled in Quincy, Illinois. Augustus spent a lot of time playing across the street from Saint Peter's Church. Augustus started attending Saint Peter's parish school. He was an excellent student and also became an altar server.

One day, several years later, Augustus was praying in church. Father McGill sat down next to him and asked Augustus if he had ever thought about becoming a priest. Augustus was surprised — that was exactly what he had been praying about! Father McGill helped Augustus apply to a

AUGUSTUS SAID:
"The Catholic Church deplores a double slavery — that of the mind and that of the body. She endeavors to free us of both."

couple of seminaries. But at this time in American history, none of the seminaries had ever had a Black priest, and every single one was afraid to let Augustus in. Augustus was very disappointed, but he didn't give up hope. He knew that the Church was run by flawed humans. People make mistakes and sometimes do bad things. He also knew that the Church belonged to Jesus and that Jesus would make sure that things would change in his Church. He believed that Jesus would find a way for him to be a priest, and so he kept praying.

Augustus was eventually accepted into a seminary in Rome, Italy. Once again, he was a wonderful student. His teachers and fellow students all loved and respected him. He learned to speak English, German, Italian, Latin, Greek, and African dialects. He had a beautiful singing voice and became an accomplished musician. After six years of study, Augustus was ordained a priest. He thought he was going to be sent to be a missionary in Africa, but in fact, he was going to be a different kind of missionary. He was sent back to Quincy. He was to be the first Black priest in America!

Newspapers told the story of the former slave boy who had become a priest in Rome. Thousands of people, both Black and White, were there to greet the new Father Tolton when he returned to his hometown. A brass band played hymns and spirituals while the Catholics followed their new priest into the church. Everyone wanted the new priest's blessing, but the first one in line was Father McGill. The next day, Augustus said Mass to a standing-room-only crowd. Father Augustus became known for his dynamic homilies and people came from all over to hear him. Unfortunately, racial prejudice and jealousy were still present in Quincy. Augustus was insulted and lied about until finally he was sent to Chicago to care for a Black parish there.

Augustus was put in charge of Saint Augustine's mission church, which met in the basement of another church. It was in a poor neighborhood made up mostly of ex-slaves. Augustus went to work. He raised money to build a church to serve the Black community. The church, Saint Monica's, grew from thirty parishioners to six hundred! Augustus gathered donations for the poor and hungry. But most of all, he ministered to those who had given up on life. He did his best to give them the hope of

Jesus, telling them that God's love is bigger and stronger than any hurt or injustice that man can do. He was a living example of Christ's love. His parishioners loved him and called him "Good Father Gus." Augustus stayed at Saint Monica's until his death.

Augustus faced prejudice, anger, and danger just because of the color of his skin. He also knew that Jesus had overcome the world and would never abandon his Church. He had faith that the Lord would help his Church to change and do the right thing. Augustus also knew that he had to be brave and step up if things were going to change. He returned love for anger, and by his courage and perseverance, blazed the way for more Black priests in America.

VENERABLE

FULL NAME:
Augustus Tolton

N **NICKNAME:**
The Trailblazer

Y **YEARS:** 1854–1897

C **COUNTRY:** United States

For things to change, someone has to be the first to stand. Someone has to stand against injustice and prejudice and fight for what is good and true. Someone has to blaze the way. You can be that someone! Sit with someone in the cafeteria who is alone. Stand up for someone who is being bullied or made fun of. Speak up and work against all types of discrimination. Be the person who says no, and helps others say no, instead of giving in to peer pressure. Let Augustus inspire you to be the first, to bravely stand and make a difference!

17
BERNARD

The Swordsman

*He could beat anyone in sword fighting and was known
as the "finest blade in Sicily," but he wanted more!*

In 1605, Bernard of Corleone was born as Filippo Latini in Corleone, Italy. His parents were faithful Catholics, and Bernard learned a love for the Mass and a desire to help the poor at an early age. When he was old enough, Bernard trained as a shoemaker like his father. But making shoes wasn't what Bernard really liked to do. He liked to swordfight!

There was a garrison near Bernard's house. There he learned to fence and duel. Bernard also had a quick temper. At any insult, real or imagined, he would draw his sword and challenge the other man. He dueled so ferociously and skillfully that soon he got the reputation of being the greatest swordsman in Sicily. He used his sword to defend the helpless and the old, but would also take on any challenger. Finally, a hired killer who thought of himself as a great swordsman challenged Bernard. Their fierce duel ended with Bernard injuring the killer's hand so badly that the arm had to be amputated.

Bernard felt horrified at what he had done. He begged forgiveness of the injured man who eventually became his friend. This incident enabled Bernard to learn to control his temper Slowly his vocation matured, and eight years later he joined the Capuchin order, taking the name Bernard. The Capuchin's are a reformed Franciscan order. When Bernard became a Capuchin, he laid down his sword forever.

BERNARD SAID:
"It is not good to leave the Blessed Sacrament alone. I will keep him company until the other friars arrive."

SAINT

FULL NAME:
Bernard of Corleone

N NICKNAME:
The Swordsman

Y YEARS: 1605–1667

C COUNTRY: Italy

Bernard put the same energy into being a friar as he had into sword fighting. Even though he had been very famous and respected as a swordsman, now he wanted only to serve others with no special treatment for himself. He became the friary cook. He had a great devotion to the Blessed Mother and built a little altar in the kitchen to pray to Mary while he cooked. He also did the laundry and took care of the sick.

Instead of letting his temper have free rein, Bernard tried to be patient and caring. He fasted and prayed to make up for the anger and violence he had shown in his old life. After midnight, when the friars finished their prayers in front of the Blessed Sacrament, Bernard would often stay, giving up sleep to spend time with Jesus. His fellow friars respected and loved Bernard. They were impressed and inspired by his holiness and gentleness. They went to Bernard for prayers and advice, and Bernard always did whatever he could to help them. When earthquakes and hurricanes hit, Bernard stayed in front of the tabernacle, praying for the Lord to have mercy until all of his brother friars were safe.

Bernard felt God calling him to help the poor and sick. When an epidemic hit the town, everyone was sick. Bernard worked night and day, helping until he himself became very ill. The doctor said that he would be dead by the next day. Bernard took a statue of Saint Francis, put it in his sleeve, and started praying that Saint Francis would heal him. He said he would not remove that statue until he was well again. When the doctor returned the next day, he expected to declare Bernard dead. Instead, Bernard was sitting up in bed. When the doctor asked what miracle medicine Bernard had taken, Bernard took the statue from his sleeve and smiled.

Bernard's desire to help the sick even included animals. People brought their sick animals to him for healing. Bernard made the Sign of the Cross over the animals and led them around the big cross that stood in front of the friary, and the animal would be healed! Some days, the other friars would complain because the yard of the friary was so filled with horses, cows, donkeys, and other sick animals.

From being a man quick to anger and violence, Bernard became the kind, gentle friar who was never seen to lose his temper or say anything bad against anyone. He lived out his life in penance, prayer, and the service of others. As he grew closer to God, he received visions of Jesus and Mary. In one of the visions, Mary told him when he would die. When that day arrived, he was given the last sacraments. Then he was heard to joyously say, "Let's go, let's go!"

Today, everyone wants to be famous. They will do anything to get on the television or internet. Bernard was famous. He was even called the greatest swordsman in the land. Yet when he took the time to think about his life and his soul, he realized that all that fame was worth nothing at all. He chose instead to follow Jesus and live the Gospel. He found the joy and peace that he had never experienced when he was a famous swordfighter.

What is important in your life? What are you spending all your time and energy on? Is it making you and your world better, and bringing you closer to God? Talk to Bernard. He'll help you figure it out!

18
PIER GIORGIO

The Terror

Known for his wicked sense of humor and inventive pranks, this mountain-climbing, Eucharist-loving athlete became a champion for the poor.

In 1901, Pier Giorgio Frassati was born in Turin, Italy. His father was a rich publisher of a liberal newspaper and a politician who didn't believe in religion. His mother, an artist, was a strict parent who passed on her Catholic faith to her son and daughter. From the beginning, Pier Giorgio wanted to help the poor. As a boy, Pier Giorgio saw a poor child with no shoes and immediately took off his own shoes and gave them to the child. He was also a very prayerful child. When he was sent to a Jesuit school, Pier Giorgio received the holy Eucharist every day (at that time, he had to receive special permission for daily Communion). He prayed the Rosary every night. Sometimes his father would come in and find him asleep on his knees, rosary in his hand.

But Pier Giorgio didn't spend all his time praying. He loved being outdoors and participated in all kinds of sports. He enjoyed riding horses, hiking, skiing, and swimming. Most of all, he loved mountain climbing. He said, "The higher we go, the better we shall hear the voice of Christ." His hikes were timed so that he could attend Mass in a little mountain church. His love of being high in the mountains led to his follow-

> **PIER GIORGIO SAID:**
> "I urge you with all the strength of my soul to approach the Eucharist Table as often as possible. Feed on this Bread of the Angels from which you will draw the strength to fight inner struggles."

ers taking up his saying, "*Verso L'alto!* To the heights!"

Pier Giorgio grew up to be the life of the party. He was the center and leader of any group he was in, initiating lots of laughter and discussions. He also loved practical jokes. Sending an important-looking package that was full of a large chunk of melting ice cream to a teacher, shortsheeting his friends' beds, waking his friends early and loudly with a toy trumpet — these were just some of his pranks. Another time, he actually managed to get a live donkey into a friend's bed! No surprise that his nickname was "The Terror"!

When he was seventeen, Pier Giorgio joined the Saint Vincent de Paul Society, an international network of friends who help people in need. He was also a lay Dominican and a member of Catholic Action, an association of Catholics that teaches how to live a Catholic Christian way of life. Pier Giorgio always put his beliefs into action. He was known for his energy and enthusiasm, and he loved and defended his faith and his people. Once, during a Church-organized protest against fascism and police violence, he saw that one of the guards had knocked the group's banner down. Pier Giorgio picked the banner up, held it even higher, and used it to block the blows of the guards against his fellow protesters.

Most of all, Pier Giorgio loved helping the poor. He would often come home without his coat, shoes, or possessions. He would cash in his first-class train ticket and bus fare and give away the money. His father yelled at him for losing his things, and his mother scolded him for being late for dinner. They didn't know that he was giving away his things and had to run home after cashing in his train or bus tickets. He found places for the homeless to live, bought food for the hungry, and even bought a bed for a sick person. He gave away everything he could. Pier Giorgio thought about becoming a priest, but instead decided to study to be a mining engineer. He believed that he could serve Christ better among the miners.

Right before he finished his engineering degree, Pier Giorgio caught polio (poliomyelitis) — a terrible disease that can lead to total paralysis or death. In just days, he became very sick. Even then his thoughts were with his beloved poor. On the night before he died, even though his hand was paralyzed, he managed to write a message to a friend reminding him to get some medicine to a poor man that Pier Giorgio had been helping.

When it was time for Pier Giorgio's funeral Mass, his parents were shocked and surprised at what they saw. Thousands of the poor, the homeless, the unemployed, and the working people lined the street. When his parents discovered all the good their son had done in his short life, it changed their lives completely. Their troubled marriage was renewed, and Pier Giorgio's father became a Catholic.

Those same people who had lined the street for the funeral started petitioning for Pier Giorgio to become a saint. He is well on his way!

BLESSED

FULL NAME: Pier Giorgio Frassati

N NICKNAME: The Terror

Y YEARS: 1901–1925

C COUNTRY: Italy

In 1990, Pope Saint John Paul II beatified Pier Giorgio — as a young man, the pope himself had been inspired by Pier Giorgio's life story.

Everything Pier Giorgio did, he did with enthusiasm. Whether he was helping the poor, protesting for justice, or climbing mountains, he put everything he had into the effort. He knew that we have to be the change that we want to see in the world. He wants you to put everything you have into whatever you choose to do. Whether you're playing a sport, singing in the school or church choir, or just helping out, give it your all! Whatever task you are doing, no matter how small, do it with the enthusiasm of Pier Giorgio. Be a champion and light for the Church. The Church needs someone with the enthusiasm of Pier Giorgio now! Is that person you? Pier Giorgio thinks so!

19
MICHAEL

The Archangel

God's most powerful warrior!

He is an angel, not a human, but if we're talking about God's superheroes, we have to include Michael. When it comes to battling evil, Saint Michael is the guy you want by your side. Called the Prince of the Angels, he is usually pictured with a sword in his hand. His very name challenges evil. *Micha-el* means "Who is like God?" This was the cry of Michael and his army as they drove the rebellious Satan and his followers out of heaven. In the last book of the Bible, Revelation, it is predicted that there will be one great final battle with Satan where Michael will finally defeat him for good.

Until that time, Michael is still on the watch for the Devil and all of this evil works. He is still in a continuing battle with Satan, who is constantly roaming the earth seeking souls. Many people today think that the Devil doesn't exist. Today, television shows and movies like to portray him as a cool, handsome guy. Don't believe either one! The Devil does exist, and he is up to no good! People have free will to choose between good and evil. Murder, terrorism, abuse, prejudice, and bullying are just some of the evils people choose to commit with the Devil coaxing them on. He works by playing on our egos and addictions. He works through jealousy, hurtful words, abuse, obsessions, and betrayal.

POPE SAINT JOHN PAUL II SAID OF MICHAEL:
"The battle against the Devil, which is the principal task of Saint Michael the Archangel, is still being fought today because the Devil is still alive and active in the world."

He does everything he can to overcome love, break up families, and drive people away from the love of God and from each other. In 1884, Pope Leo XIII had a frightening vision of Satan. This inspired him to write the Prayer to Saint Michael:

> Saint Michael the Archangel, defend us in battle. Be our protection against the wickedness and snares of the devil. May God rebuke him, we humbly pray. And do thou, O Prince of the Heavenly Host, by the power of God, cast into hell Satan and all the evil spirits who prowl about the world seeking the ruin of souls. Amen

This powerful prayer is a great weapon against the forces of darkness. Use it as much as you can!

There are many churches and monasteries dedicated to Michael, but perhaps the most famous are the monasteries that form what is called the Sword of Saint Michael. The Sword of Saint Michael is a group of seven holy places that form a straight line from Ireland to Israel. Even more amazing, the three most important sites — Mont-Saint-Michel in France, the Sacra di San Miguel in Val di Susa, Italy, and the Sanctuary of Monte Sant'Angelo on Monte Gargano, Italy — are all the same distance one from the other. The line is also perfectly aligned with the sunset on the day of the summer solstice. Archeologists have discovered that some of the monasteries of the Sword of Saint Michael were built over pagan temples whose worshipers sought the land's high places to follow the path of the sun and to practice their rituals, which sometimes included blood or even human sacrifices. A symbol of Christianity's fight against paganism, most of the seven monasteries are linked with apparitions of, or interventions by, the fighting archangel. There is only one site, Mount Carmel, which doesn't have a direct connection with Michael, but this was a place of spiritual battle where Elijah defeated pagan prophets, and there are legends linking Elijah and Michael. The Sword of Saint Michael is a sign for us that God used his prince of the warriors to battle with the pagan forces and reclaim those sites and people for the one true God of truth and love.

One of the most famous places in the Sword of Saint Michael is Monte Sant'Angelo, on top of Monte Gargano in Italy. In the year 490, a nobleman was searching Monte Sant'Angelo for his lost prize bull. After looking for hours, he found the bull kneeling in a cave. Since he couldn't get into the cave, he decided to shoot an arrow into the cave to punish the bull for its disobedience. He shot the arrow, but to his amazement, the arrow turned around and struck the nobleman. Scared at this strange happening, the man went to his bishop and told him what had happened.

ARCHANGEL

FULL NAME:
Michael the Archangel

NICKNAME: The Warrior

The bishop ordered three days of fasting and prayer. At the end of the three days, Michael appeared to the bishop and said: "I am Michael the Archangel and am always in the presence of God. I chose the cave as sacred to me. There will be no more shedding of bull's blood. Where the rocks open widely, the sins of men may be pardoned. What is asked here in prayer will be granted. Therefore, go up to the mountain cave and dedicate it to the Christian God." A pagan Roman cult had formerly used the cave to perform rituals using bull's blood.

The bishop thought he was going crazy and tried to forget the vision. Two years later, the bishop's city was attacked by the pagans. Michael appeared to the bishop again and promised to save the city. A violent storm destroyed the attacking army. In thanksgiving, the bishop led a procession to the cave, but did not dare to enter. Michael appeared to the bishop a third time and ordered the bishop to enter the cave. Michael said: "It is not necessary that you dedicate this church that I have consecrated with my presence. Enter and pray with my assistance and celebrate the Sacrifice. I will show you how I have consecrated this place." The bishop entered the cave where he found an altar with a red cloth, a crystal cross and a footprint on the ground. It is the only building of worship in the Catholic Church that has not been consecrated by man! This cave is considered one of the holiest places in the world.

Michael made one more appearance on Monte Gargano during a plague in 1656, when the local bishop prayed to Michael for protection. Michael appeared to him and the plague disappeared. The shrine became more popular than ever. To get to the cave, visitors enter what looks like the front of a church but isn't! After walking through the front door, they are immediately faced with a long staircase that leads down into the mountain. The stairs eventually open into a marvelous church that is half cave and half man-made with dramatic skylights above. This beautiful, wonderfully unique church dedicated by Saint Michael himself has been visited by many saints and was a pilgrimage stop for the Crusaders. Saint Francis considered it to be so holy that he wouldn't even enter the cave, and only prayed outside. Padre Pio lived nearby and also visited the holy site. At least seven popes have visited, including JP2 and Pope Benedict XVI.

Michael and his fellow angels are there whenever you need them. You just have to ask. There are many cases of people being protected and saved by Michael and his angels. Some have even seen him, sword and all, or have later found out that an attacker was scared off by a large man in white (only seen by the attacker) walking next to them!

Whenever you are in danger, facing evil, or just feeling scared, ask Michael to fight for you. Today, many people do not follow God's will. When you see evil things happening in your family, country, or even the world, ask Michael to help you fight and reclaim those souls in the name of Jesus for the glory of God. Remember, he's God's warrior!

Missale
Romanum

Gloria in excelsis
...

20
JRR

The Author

He wrote The Hobbit *and* The Lord of the Rings —
*but did you know that the stories and characters he
created were greatly inspired by his Catholic faith?*

John Ronald Reuel (JRR) Tolkien was born in 1892 in Bloemfontein, South Africa. His family moved to England three years later. The next year, JRR's father died of rheumatic fever. Several years later, JRR's mother, Mabel, became a Catholic along with her sister, May. Mabel then had both of her sons, JRR and Hilary, baptized. Her Baptist family was not happy about her conversion and cut off all financial support. Because of this, the little family was very poor. Mabel struggled to earn enough food for her family while also suffering from diabetes. Four years later, when JRR was twelve, Mabel died. Later in life, JRR said that he considered his mother a martyr who had offered her life so that her sons might know the true Catholic Faith. Before she died, Mabel arranged for her close priest friend Father Francis to become her sons' guardian. JRR grew to love and respect him. JRR went on to study and get a degree in English language and literature.

In 1915, JRR joined the British Army to fight in World War I. He fought in the Battle of the

JRR SAID:
"We have come from God and inevitably the myths woven by us, though they contain error, will also reflect a splintered fragment of the true light, the eternal truth that is with God. Indeed, only by myth-making, only by becoming a 'sub-creator' and inventing stories, can man ascribe to the state of perfection that he knew before the Fall."

DAD

FULL NAME:
JRR Tolkien

N **NICKNAME:** The Author
Y **YEARS:** 1892–1973
C **COUNTRY:** England

Somme, in which one million men were wounded or killed. He felt that their deaths gave him a great obligation to do good and do God's will in the world. Right after that battle, JRR contracted trench fever and spent the rest of the war in hospitals and doing desk jobs.

During the war, he fell in love with a young woman named Edith, his childhood sweetheart, and married her. They had fifty-five happy years together! They went on to have three sons and one daughter. JRR loved being a father and tried to spend as much time with his family as possible. He wanted to make sure that his children knew that he loved them, and he did his best to make sure his work didn't interfere with his family time. He strove to pass on to his children the Catholic Faith that had been so important to his mother. At bedtime, JRR would entertain his children by telling marvelous stories of elves, dragons, and hobbits. They loved the stories so much that he wrote them down and even drew illustrations to go with them.

After the war, JRR became a professor of English literature at Oxford University. It was at Oxford that JRR met and formed a life-long friendship with C. S. Lewis. Lewis encouraged his friend to take his hobby of writing fiction and work toward a book that could be published. JRR took the bedtime stories that had so fascinated his kids, reworked them, and published *The Hobbit,* followed by *The Lord of the Rings.* While he was writing, he also continued practicing the Faith that had become so important to him. He regularly attended Mass and had a great devotion to the Blessed Sacrament. He told one of his sons, "I put before you the one great thing to love on earth: the Blessed Sacrament. ... There you will find romance, glory, honor, fidelity, and the true way of all your loves on earth." He even translated the Our Father, Hail Mary, and some of the other traditional Catholic prayers into one of his invented languages from *The Lord of the Rings*, Quenya!

JRR wanted his stories to bring people into an encounter with truth and beauty. His books are filled with model's of virtuous men and women who inspire us.

His faith influenced and was the source of inspiration for everything JRR did. As an author, he used his stories to reflect the values and truths of his faith. JRR always said that all good stories hold up a mirror and show us who we are. He hoped that his books would do just that, and inspire people to live a life closer to God. In his books, he hoped to show us how good always overcomes evil, that light always overcomes the darkness. Most of all, JRR wanted to be a good father and pass on his Catholic faith. Even when he got older and his children moved away, JRR would write them letter after letter, encouraging them and giving them advice on how to live life and deal with trials as a Christian in this modern world. If someday you become a parent or have an opportunity to influence a young person, remember JRR! By the way he spent his life and passed on his faith, he lived his vocation as husband and father to the fullest and used the gifts God gave him. He became a light in the world and tried his best to help his children become lights too. By his example and through his characters, JRR invites you to enter this great adventure of life, to pass on your faith to others, to fight evil, and to be a light to the world!

21
PAUL

The Evangelizer

*He hated Christians so much that he spent his time tracking
them down and having them executed, yet God chose
him to become one of our Church's greatest apostles.*

Paul, who was also called Saul, was born in Tarsus, in modern Turkey, around the same time as Jesus was born. He was sent to Jerusalem for school and ended up staying there. He became a respected scholar and member of the Jewish Pharisee religious party. After the death and resurrection of Jesus, more and more people were becoming Christian. Paul believed that Christianity was a false religion, and became obsessed with stopping it. It became his mission to hunt down these new Christians. He had them dragged out of their homes, beaten, and imprisoned. He approved and participated in the stoning to death of Stephen, the first Christian martyr. Paul continued his persecutions of the Christians, until one fateful day on the road to Damascus.

Paul was traveling on one of his missions to discover and destroy Christians. Suddenly, he was blinded by a bright light. He fell to the ground and heard a voice say, "Saul, Saul, why do you persecute me?" Paul cried out, "Who are you, Lord?" The voice replied, "I am Jesus, whom you are persecuting; but rise and enter the city, and you will be told what you are to do" (Acts 9:4–6).

Paul got up, but found that he was blind. The men who were traveling with him led him into the city of Damascus. He stayed there three days, not eating or

PAUL SAID:
"I can do all things through him who strengthens me!" (Phil 4:13)

drinking, until a Christian man named Ananias came to see him. Jesus had appeared to Ananias and told him to go visit Paul and pray over him. So Ananias prayed over Paul. Suddenly, Paul could see again! Paul was baptized and began to eat and drink. Soon he had his strength back.

Now Paul's real mission began. He began to preach that Jesus was the Son of God. This shocked everyone who had known Paul as a persecutor of Christians. His dynamic words inspired and converted many, but those who still hated the Christians plotted to kill Paul. Paul traveled to Jerusalem. He went to join the apostles, but they were all still afraid of him. Finally, they realized that Paul had truly converted. Paul stayed with them and began to preach. After finding out there was another plot to kill him, the apostles sent Paul back to Tarsus. It was then that Paul set to work.

Paul traveled the world preaching and writing. He was known as the "Apostle to the Gentiles" — any people who were not Jewish. When Christianity first began to spread, the original apostles thought that in order to be baptized, converts would have to become Jewish first. Paul argued against this and won. Paul spent most of his time in foreign lands bringing the Christian Faith to everyone.

Paul traveled to Arabia, Asia, Europe, and back to Jerusalem and Rome. He was fearless in his enthusiasm for spreading the word and converting people to Christianity. As driven as he had been persecuting Christians, he was even more determined to spread the news of the risen Jesus. He was the main force in bringing the Good News to the Gentiles, those people who were not of the Jewish faith. Through all his travels, Paul kept in touch with different communities of Christians. He sent them letters full of advice and settled their disagreements. These letters — also called epistles — were saved and read over and over by the new Christians. Despite shipwrecks, beatings, imprisonments, exhausting travels, danger, hunger, and persecution, Paul carried out God's mission. Finally, thinking that was the only way to stop him, the Romans executed him. They were wrong! Paul's mission had only just begun.

Paul brought Jesus to the world. He knew that the message of Jesus was for everyone. The communities of Christians he started spread like wildfire. His letters became part of the Bible and are read at Mass. Through his letters, he continues to inspire and challenge us today. Paul didn't let hardship, threats, violence, or shipwrecks stop him. He wants you to help him take up the cause. He needs you to spread the news of Jesus in your corner of the world. The world today tries to make Christianity look outdated and unnecessary. Nothing is further from the truth! With all the trouble in today's world, people need Jesus more than ever! Paul needs you to continue his mission of spreading the Gospel to the world. He knows you may face opposition, criticism, and even hostility when you do. He knows the forces of darkness will be against you.

Be inspired by this advice that Paul gave in the Bible:

SAINT

FULL NAME: Paul of Tarsus

N NICKNAME: The Evangelizer

Y YEARS: 3–65

C COUNTRY: Turkey, Italy, Syria, Greece, Asia

Therefore take the whole armor of God, that you may be able to withstand in the evil day, and having done all, to stand. Stand therefore, having fastened the belt of truth around your waist, and having put on the breastplate of righteousness, and having shod your feet with the equipment of the gospel of peace; besides all these, taking the shield of faith, with which you can quench all the flaming darts of the Evil One. And take the helmet of salvation, and the sword of the Spirit, which is the word of God. (Ephesians 6:10–17)

22
MIKE

The Baseball Player

*The son of poor Irish immigrants, he became a beloved,
baseball-playing priest and founded the Knights of
Columbus, a global fraternity that has helped millions!*

Born in 1852 in Waterbury, Connecticut, Michael McGivney was the son of poor Irish immigrants. Mike was the oldest of 13 children! Life was not easy back then for Irish Catholic immigrants. Their neighbors, who were mostly Protestant, looked down on them as ignorant, dirty puppets of the pope, looking to take over their good neighborhoods. Many signs advertising jobs or places for rent would include the phrase "No Irish Need Apply!" The government of Connecticut tried to prevent Catholic churches from being built in the state. Because of this prejudice, the Irish had to take the lowest-paid, least-wanted jobs. Despite all the prejudice and hardship, the Irish immigrants drew strength from their Catholic faith. At home and in church, Mike learned about sacrifice, love, and prayer.

Mike was an exceptional student. He graduated school three years early at the young age of thirteen, and got a job in the spoon-making department of a brass factory to help support his family. Mike worked there for three years until he managed to convince his father to let him enter the seminary to become a priest. At the age of sixteen, Mike answered God's call and began his studies. He studied in Canada and New York for four years. His dedication, ho-

MIKE SAID:
"Although but a few years organized, the Order has effected incalculable good in many households!"

105

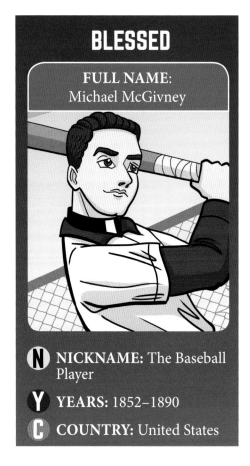

BLESSED

FULL NAME:
Michael McGivney

N **NICKNAME:** The Baseball Player

Y **YEARS:** 1852–1890

C **COUNTRY:** United States

liness, and humor impressed everyone he met. Then tragedy struck when Mike's father suddenly died. Mike returned home immediately, thinking that he might have to give up his dream of becoming a priest and go back to the factory to support the family. But after hearing of Mike's situation, the bishop of Hartford provided financial assistance that enabled Mike to return to the seminary, this time in Maryland. Once again, Mike's holiness, dedication, and humor made him popular in the seminary.

Besides his studies and duties as a seminarian, Mike also kept busy playing the fairly new sport of baseball. He and his fellow seminarians formed a team called the Charter Oaks. In a reported May 20, 1872, game against another seminary team, the Mohawks, Mike started in left field. Playing this position meant he had to be a fast runner and have a good throwing arm. He also batted cleanup and scored three times, ultimately leading his team to victory.

After completing his seminary studies, Mike was ordained in 1877. He was assigned as assistant priest at Saint Mary's Church, the first Catholic church in New Haven, Connecticut. The new assignment was full of challenges. Mike faced the debt of building the new church, the difficulty of caring for the many illnesses and needs common among the poor immigrants of his congregation, as well as a pastor who was in poor health. There was also the rising hostility and prejudice against Catholics. Mike had a gift for talking to people, and began the difficult task of inspiring his discouraged congregation and negotiating with antagonistic neighbors. He became known for his wise advice and wonderful homilies.

Mike ministered to everyone in need. While visiting a prison, he got to know a twenty-one-year-old man named Chip Smith, who had been convicted of shooting a police officer while drunk. Chip had been sentenced to death by hanging. Mike began to visit this young man. He talked with him and prayed with him, and Chip returned to the sacraments. The guards were amazed at the improvement in the young man's behavior and his change of heart. On the day of the execution, Mike said Mass for Chip one last time and then walked by his side to the gallows.

Mike set to work building a church community. He organized plays, parish fairs, and, of course, baseball games. He founded groups to fight the growing problem of alcoholism. He understood the needs and problems of the Irish immigrant community because he had lived them. With enthusiastic ideas and a ready laugh, he tried to lift the spirits of his parish and bring them together as a family.

At this time, there was not much help for the poor. Widows whose husbands died were left in extreme poverty. They had no safety net to support them and were often at risk of having their children confiscated by the government and placed in institutions. Mike knew firsthand about the fear and desperation that came when a family lost their father who was the main provider. He became determined to help these families. He came up with the idea of forming a mutual aid order that would provide help and money for widows and orphans. The members of this order would be the men of the parish. They would form a fraternity, a group of men who would not only support the needs of the community, but would also encourage and inspire each other as brothers. In the face of prejudice and persecution, this brotherhood would help its members stay strong in their faith and enable them to face the hardships of life together. The organization would also improve the life of Irish families. Mike wanted the order to promote unity and charity.

Mike suggested using Columbus as their patron. At the time, Columbus was considered a hero in America for discovering the New World. He was also a Catholic. So, by choosing the name The Knights of Columbus, Mike hoped to give the new order a strong American Catholic identity. He wanted the order to help families stay together and stay Catholic. This eventually expanded to include all kinds of charitable work. Today, there are more than 16,000 active councils of the Knights of Columbus all over the world! Over 2 million Knights are volunteering their time and talent as brothers to help those in need and promote the Catholic Faith. Knights greet each other with the words "*Vivat Jesus!*" which means "Jesus lives!" Showing that Jesus is alive and cares for his people is the heart and mission of the order that Mike founded.

After seven years at Saint Mary's, Mike was transferred to pastor at Saint Thomas Church in Thomaston.

Once again, he got to work building a church community by organizing plays and church fairs. Of course, he started up a baseball team and even coached third base. He also established several councils of the Knights of Columbus. He had electricity and a telephone installed in the rectory, and even got a parish dog. In 1890, Mike came down with the Russian flu, a pandemic now considered by many scientists to be a coronavirus. It developed into pneumonia and on August 14, 1890, Mike died. He was beatified in 2020, the last step before sainthood. If canonized, Mike could become the first man born in the United States and the first Irish American to become a saint!

Mike never gave up. No matter what challenges came his way, he faced them with faith, determination, and enthusiasm. He always made himself available to anyone in need. He answered God's call, and not only did he change the lives of his parishioners, but also, through the order he started, he has helped millions more and has changed the world. God does not always go looking for those who are most qualified. Sometimes God just needs someone available and willing. Make yourself available. Step up! Volunteer at a food pantry, animal shelter, or wherever there is a need. Join the Squires (the Knights' youth fraternity for ages ten to eighteen), and then become a Knight. (There is a Knights auxiliary for women, too!) Consider making a difference in the world by becoming a priest or religious! Whatever you do, do it to the best of your ability and with a smile. When problems come your way, don't give up! Ask Mike to help you figure it out and then keep going. A smile and a positive attitude can turn any job into a witness for Jesus! Make people want to know what gives you that smile. Make yourself available to God. Be like Mike and watch what happens! *Vivat Jesus!*

P.S. Next time you're watching a baseball game, pray a quick hi to Mike!

23
THOMAS

The Teacher

*Called a "dumb ox" by his classmates, he became one
of the Church's most famous writers and teachers.*

Born around 1225 in the family castle in Roccasecca, Italy, Thomas Aquinas was one of nine children and the youngest boy in the family. His mother, the countess of Teano, was told by a prayerful hermit that this new son would become a great student and a Dominican priest. But after hearing this, his parents decided that they wanted him to become a Benedictine priest instead of a Dominican. The Dominicans were a new order and begged to support themselves, while the Benedictines had a more prominent and well-off position in the Church and society. So when he was five years old, Thomas was sent to learn at a Benedictine abbey. While at the abbey, young Thomas surprised the monks by constantly asking, "What is God?"

After completing his education with the Benedictines, Thomas began studying at the University of Naples. While there, he joined the Dominican order. When his family found out, they were furious. They kidnapped him and held him captive for a year, trying to persuade him to give up being a Dominican. Thomas held firm. During this year, Saint Thomas tutored his younger sister in philosophy, theology, and the Dominican life. After a year, Saint Thomas escaped with the help of his mother and fled to the Do-

> **THOMAS SAID:**
> "We must love them both, those whose opinions we share and those whose opinions we reject, for both have labored in the search for truth, and both have helped us in finding it."

minicans in Naples. Thomas remained a Dominican and was sent to study at the Universities of Paris and Cologne. His teacher was Saint Albert the Great, who you met earlier. Because Thomas was a big guy who was awkward and shy, other students teased him and called him a "dumb ox." However, Albert could see the brilliance of this quiet student and told them, "You call him the dumb ox, but in his teaching, he will one day produce such a bellowing that it will be heard throughout the world."

Albert was right. Soon, Thomas was writing, lecturing, and teaching. Among other topics, he helped people understand the relationship between faith (theology) and reason (philosophy). He taught that since both the study of God and the study of natural things came from God, faith and reason worked together. Thomas said that reason could make faith easier to understand, and faith could guide reason and keep it from making mistakes. Thomas also taught that the existence of God could be proved through reason alone and also could be accepted through faith. He wrote many works on the Bible and the Church Fathers, as well as beautiful hymns. Thomas's most famous work is the *Summa Theologica*, a tremendous work made up of three parts, which are divided into ten treatises, which answer 614 different theological questions, and address around ten thousand objections. (The objections are where he gives and responds to arguments against his answers to the questions.) In the *Summa*, Thomas discussed the nature of God, God's relationship with man and creation, and the Catholic Church, among many other theological topics.

In 1273, Saint Thomas was seen by the sacristan levitating and crying while praying before an icon of the crucifix in the Chapel of Saint Nicholas. When asked, Thomas said that he had had a vision. In his vision, he heard a voice coming from the crucifix that said, "Thou hast written well of me, Thomas; what reward wilt thou have?" Thomas replied, "None other than thyself, Lord." During Mass that day, Thomas was then given a revelation from God, a glimpse of eternity. After this vision, Thomas stopped writing, leaving the *Summa* unfinished. When asked why, he replied, "I can do no more. The end of my labors has come. Such things I have seen and such things have been revealed to me that all I have written seems as so much straw." After his vision, Thomas felt that no one, let alone himself, could come close to describing the infinite glory of God. He never wrote again and died from an illness several months later. He was declared a saint and named a Doctor of the Church.

Thomas inspires us to think. Critics of Catholics like to say that we are blind believers who follow the Church without reason. This couldn't be further from the truth. Some of the greatest philosophers, theologians, and scientists have been people of faith. Explore your faith, read books on history, theology, philosophy, and the Catholic Faith,

SAINT

FULL NAME:
Thomas Aquinas

NICKNAME: The Teacher
YEARS: 1225–1274
COUNTRY: Italy

because the truth always leads to God himself. We may not be able to comprehend the total infinite power and glory of God, but thanks to teachers like Thomas, we can get an idea!

24
JOHN

The Magician

He was God's magician, who used his circus skills
to make a difference in the lives of others.

John Bosco was born in Becchi, Italy, in 1815. War, famine, and drought made this a really bad time to grow up in Italy. Even worse, his father died when John was only two. John grew up helping on the family farm and going to church regularly. When he was nine years old, he had a dream of a wild group of poor boys who were swearing and fighting. In the dream were a princely-looking man and a noble woman. The man told John that he could help these friends of his, not by hitting and yelling, but with kindness and gentleness. Then the woman told him that should be strong and humble, and that he would understand all of this in time.

Not long after the dream, a traveling circus came to town. John was fascinated with the acrobats, jugglers, and magicians. They were amazing! He also thought that this would be a good way to attract the attention of others. He watched the performers carefully until he learned how to do their tricks. Then he put on his own performances for the neighborhood kids. After the performance, he would recite the homily he had heard that day. He did this several times until he realized that he wanted to become a priest himself.

His older brother was real-

JOHN SAID:
"If one is to do good, he must have a little courage, be ready for sacrifice, deal affably with all, and never slight anybody. By following this method I have always had significant success. In fact, marvelous success."

SAINT

FULL NAME:
John Bosco

N **NICKNAME:**
The Magician

Y **YEARS:** 1815–1888

C **COUNTRY:** Italy

ly angry at the idea. He gave John a beating, hoping to change his mind, and told him to be a farmer like the rest of the family. Undeterred, John decided to leave home and find a job until he was old enough to become a priest. He was only twelve when he went out on his own! There was another obstacle in his way. John needed an education if he wanted to get into a seminary. Luckily, he found a priest who was willing to teach him. After several years of working at a vineyard and studying, John entered the seminary.

John became a priest and was sent to the city of Turin, where there were many slums and poor people. When John visited the prison, he was shocked to see how many young boys, twelve to eighteen years old, were inside that terrible place. John felt called to do something to help the other boys from ending up there.

John went out into the streets to try to talk to the boys who were getting into trouble, but they wanted nothing to do with him. Then he remembered how his friends used to love his juggling and magic performances. He studied, practiced, and then went back out and started performing magic tricks for the street kids. This gave John the chance he was looking for. Once he got their attention with his tricks, he would talk to them about God and how the Lord cared about them and wanted more for their lives. Boys started to trust this performing priest and came to him with their problems. Many of the boys were homeless, so John would find places for them to stay. His mother came to live with him and help him, and she became affectionately known as Mama Margherita. Soon Mama Margherita and Don Bosco (Father Bosco) were taking care of almost eight hundred boys!

John tried to find jobs for all the boys. At that time, it was common for boys to be beaten or worked extremely hard with no time off, doing all kinds of hard work. John talked to employers and had contracts made so that the boys would be treated fairly with no beatings. He started a school to train boys in job skills. The school also had classes to educate the boys in art, science, and religion. John wanted to design a school system that was based on "reason, religion, and kindness." Remembering the dream that he had when he was nine, he didn't yell or hit the boys. Instead, he treated them with the kindness and respect they had never experienced before in their lives.

Some of the boys wanted to follow John and become priests, so he started another school to help them. Then he realized that he needed help caring for all the homeless and needy boys and that he needed to prepare for his work to go on after he was gone. So he started an order of priests, called the Society of St. Francis de Sales (or Salesians), and an order of Salesian sisters to help poor and needy girls.

John continued his work until he died in 1888. Today, there are thousands of Salesians helping young people all over the world!

John found a way to reach those boys in need by using his talents as a performer. In fact, he is considered the first to use what is now called "Gospel Magic," the use of stage magic to spread the message of Jesus. God uses everything! John also knew that yelling and violence never helps. He used love and kindness instead to help and overcome. Instead of letting a fight explode, remember John, stay calm, and switch tactics. Find your talents and use them creatively to make the world a better place. And do it with a smile!

25
MAX

The Knight

Devoted to Mother Mary, this Knight of Our Lady fought to spread the word of God and the love of Our Lady until he faced the ultimate challenge in a Nazi death camp.

Originally named Raymund, Max was born in Zduńska Wola, Poland in 1894. He loved to play pranks and was constantly getting into trouble. Finally, his mother just yelled at him, "I don't know what will become of you!" Max felt terrible. He didn't mean to be bad, it just sort of happened. He decided to pray to Mother Mary. Ever since he was very small, Max had always had a special love for Our Lady. So he knelt and prayed very hard to know what would happen to him.

Mary came to him in a vision and offered him two crowns, one red and one white: the white one for purity, meaning he would stay pure and become a priest, and the red one for martyrdom, meaning that he would die for the Faith. Max said, "I choose both." From then on, he dedicated his life to God through Mary.

He became a Franciscan priest, which was when he received the name Maximilian. He was sent to Rome to study and received a doctorate in theology and philosophy. In Rome, he started the Knights of the Immaculata, an organization open to all Catholics. The Knights pray and work to bring

MAX SAID:
"Let us give every difficulty, every sorrow to her [Mary], and have confidence that she will take care of it better than we could. Peace then, peace, much peace in an unlimited confidence in her. ... Above all, never let yourselves be troubled, never be frightened, never fear anything."

people to God and defeat evil through the intercession of Mary, especially by praying the Rosary. Through the years, the Rosary has been called one of the most powerful prayers by saints and popes. In fact, most people in religious orders wear their rosary on the left side, because that is the side where a sword is traditionally worn. Their "sword," the rosary, is a most formidable weapon against evil! Today there are thousands of members of the Knights of the Immaculata throughout the world.

Max returned to Poland and began to evangelize. He started a religious publishing press and helped produce a radio show. He traveled to India and Japan and founded monasteries there. He continued to work until his health made him return home.

When the German Nazi army invaded Poland, Max fought against the brutal Nazi regime by publishing anti-Nazi articles. He and his fellow friars hid 2,000 Jews in the monastery to save them from persecution and arrest. Finally, the German authorities shut down Max's monastery. Max and four other friars were arrested. They were sent to the death camp, Auschwitz.

Max didn't let being in the camp stop him from being a priest. He continued to minister to his fellow prisoners. This made the guards very angry. Max was constantly beaten and harassed. But he continued.

Then one day, a prisoner escaped. The camp officials decided that they would pick ten prisoners and starve them to death in order to discourage anyone else from trying to escape. They randomly picked ten men. One of the men began to cry and beg for his life. He had a wife and children who needed him. Immediately, Max volunteered to take his place. He and the other nine men were locked in a bunker without food or water. Max led the men in prayer and comforted them. The guards had expected the men to yell, curse, and despair. They were shocked to hear the men singing hymns and praying. One by one, the men died of starvation and thirst. After two weeks, Max was the only one left alive. The guards injected him with poison and Max died.

Max's devotion to Mary guided his whole life. He invites you to join with him in this devotion to our Mother in heaven. Jesus gave us Mary as our Mother. She is always there to love and care for us. Go to her with your worries and problems. She is a woman of courage, strength, caring, and love. Some people say that it's wrong that Catholics pay so much attention to Mary, and they even claim that we worship her. But we don't worship her. Catholics only worship God. We simply honor Mary as the Mother of God. When we pray to her, it's like going to our own mother and asking her to pray to Jesus for us. What son would be angry that people honored his mother? As Max said: "Never be afraid of loving the Blessed Virgin too much. You can never love her more than Jesus did."

As a Knight of Our Lady, Max fought against evil and

SAINT

FULL NAME:
Maximilian Kolbe

N **NICKNAME:** The Knight
Y **YEARS:** 1894–1941
C **COUNTRY:** Poland

stood for truth. He is always looking for new recruits to join the fight and make a difference. What do you think? Would you make a good knight? Mary and Max know that you would! Why not keep a rosary in your left pocket for the times when you need a spiritual weapon?

26
FULTON

The Communicator

*This brilliant bishop had his own TV show, and
was on the cover of Time magazine.*

Fulton started life out as a sickly baby with tuberculosis. Originally named Peter, he was born in El Paso, Illinois, in 1895. When he was growing up, his family started calling him Fulton, his mother's maiden name. Fulton liked the name and kept it for the rest of his life. His parents, good Irish Catholics, made sure all their children went to church. Fulton became an altar server at the Cathedral of Saint Mary in Peoria. One day he was serving at a Mass for Bishop John L. Spalding when a glass cruet full of wine slipped out of his hands. It fell to the hard floor and shattered. The wine went everywhere. Fulton was horrified and very embarrassed. After Mass, the bishop called Fulton over. Fulton was sure that the bishop would be furious with him. Instead, the bishop assured him that it was just an accident. He told Fulton that someday Fulton would study at the Catholic University in Belgium and that one day Fulton would be just like him. From that day on, Fulton knew that he was going to become a priest.

He studied at The Catholic University of America (CUA) and then traveled to study at the Catholic University in Belgium just like Bishop Spalding had said. After getting degrees in philosophy and theology, Fulton returned to America to teach at CUA. Word spread of his dynamic speaking

FULTON SAID:
"This is the choice before us: either try to revolutionize the world and break under it or revolutionize ourselves and remake the world."

VENERABLE

FULL NAME:
Fulton Sheen

N **NICKNAME:**
The Communicator

Y **YEARS:** 1895–1979

C **COUNTRY:** United States

style, and his classes were always full. He started hosting a radio show that became very popular. Then he was made a bishop and sent to New York City.

That year, Fulton began taping his television show *Life Is Worth Living*. It was an instant hit! Fulton spent the hour-long show talking about faith, God, and moral and religious issues. Fulton didn't use a script or cue cards, but would often use a blackboard to write down points and illustrate his topics. When there was no more space left on the blackboard, Fulton moved to another part of the set while asking his "angels" (members of his crew) to clean off the board. As many as thirty million viewers a week tuned in to watch Bishop Sheen. When asked about his popularity, Fulton said, "When I stand up to talk, people listen to me; they will follow what I have to say. Is it any power of mine? Of course not. Saint Paul says, 'What have you that you have not received and you who have received, why do you glory as if you had not?' But the secret of my power is that I have never in fifty-five years missed spending an hour in the presence of Our Lord in the Blessed Sacrament. That's where the power comes from."

Life and *Time* magazines did feature stories on Fulton. He also won one Emmy award for Outstanding Television Personality and was nominated for Emmy awards three times. In his Emmy acceptance speech,

Fulton thanked his four show "writers" — Matthew, Mark, Luke, and John. Through his program, Fulton educated, inspired, and converted millions of Americans.

Fulton was also appointed the national director of the Propagation of the Faith, an international association that gathers and coordinates donations to help Catholic priests, nuns, and brothers in mission areas. Through radio and television, he raised millions of dollars for the poor all over the world. He was then appointed bishop of Rochester, New York. At this time, he hosted another television show called *The Fulton Sheen Program*. He was also doing a lot of writing. Fulton wrote 73 books and many newspaper and magazine articles over his lifetime. Two months before Fulton died, Pope John Paul II (now Saint John Paul II) visited Saint Patrick's Cathedral. When the pope met Fulton, he hugged him and said: "You have written and spoken well of the Lord Jesus Christ. You are a loyal son of the Church." In 1979, Fulton died in his chapel, next to the Blessed Sacrament.

When Fulton dropped that wine cruet and watched it shatter all over the floor, he never imagined the life God had in store for him. God has amazing plans for each and every one of us. All we have to do is say yes! Do you remember where Fulton said he got his inspiration, speaking ability, and power from? Spend some time in front of the Blessed Sacrament. Wait until you see what powers Jesus will give you!

27
PIERRE

The Hairdresser

He went from a slave in Haiti, to a hairdresser to the super-rich of New York City, to a wealthy and holy businessman!

In 1766, Pierre Toussaint was born a slave on the island of Haiti. At the time, most of the slaves of Haiti were being terribly mistreated. Nearly half of all the men working in the fields died from sickness, abuse, and exhaustion before they were forty. Finally, this led to a revolt by the slaves. Violence spread through Haiti as the Black slaves fought to be free.

Pierre's owner, Jean Berard, had become wealthy from the sale of sugarcane. However, Pierre was spared from the horrors of the sugarcane fields and was raised as a house slave. Berard, a Catholic himself, had Pierre baptized and educated. (It was very unusual for slaves to be educated at this time.) Pierre was also allowed to go into the family library, where he read many Catholic classics. His favorite was *The Imitation of Christ,* which he quoted for the rest of his life.

When Pierre was twenty-one, the violence in Haiti scared Berard and his family into leaving. Berard, his wife, and five house slaves (including Pierre and his sister Rosalie) moved to New York City. At the time they arrived in New York, there were only around 300 Catholics in a city of 3,000. Most of the people didn't like Catholics. Catholics were made fun of and looked down on. Pierre didn't care. He went to Mass faithfully every day for the next sixty years.

PIERRE SAID:
"I have never felt I am a slave to any man or woman, but I am the servant of Almighty God who made us all. When one of his children is in need, I am glad to be his slave."

VENERABLE

FULL NAME:
Pierre Toussaint

N **NICKNAME:**
The Hairdresser

Y **YEARS:** 1766–1853

C **COUNTRY:** United States

In New York, Pierre was apprenticed to a hairdresser. He worked hard and found that he had a talent for styling hair. Soon Pierre was in great demand by the wealthy socialites of New York City. As he styled their hair, Pierre would often evangelize and speak to his clients about faith and God's love. Word spread of this talented, caring stylist, and Pierre started making good money.

After hearing that his plantation back in Haiti had been burned to the ground and his fortune was lost, a shocked and weakened Jean Berard died of pleurisy. This left his wife, Marie, alone and penniless. Instead of leaving, Pierre worked harder. By working sixteen-hour days, he earned enough money to support Berard's widow, Pierre's sister Rosalie, and the other slaves. Soon he had enough to buy Rosalie's freedom. During this time, Pierre fell in love with Juliette Noel, another Haitian slave living in New York. Marie Berard eventually fell ill and finally freed Pierre before she died. He had saved enough to buy the freedom of his fiancée, Juliette, and four years later they married.

Pierre and Juliette were married for forty happy years. When yellow fever, a terrible disease that was very contagious, raged through the city, Pierre risked his own health to care for people who had been abandoned because others feared catching the disease. Armed with a Bible and a rosary, he would go into infected homes to nurse the sick no matter who they were. When

Pierre's sister Rosalie died, Pierre and Juliette adopted her daughter, Euphemie. Pierre continued to work as a hairdresser and invested his money in banks and real estate. As his business grew, Pierre became a wealthy man, but he kept working. He said, "I have enough for myself, but if I stop working I have not enough for others." He bought the freedom of more slaves and helped them find jobs. Immigrants, especially those coming from Haiti, knew they could come to Pierre for anything they needed.

Through everything, Pierre continued to go to daily Mass and Eucharistic adoration. He taught catechism to adults and children. Pierre and Juliette were instrumental in founding Saint Mark the Evangelist Catholic School in Harlem, the first New York Catholic school for Black children. They opened their home to orphans and young people in need. They donated to Saint Elizabeth Seton's religious order, school, and orphanage. They also supported the work and orphanage of the Oblate Sisters of Providence, the first community of Black religious women in the United States.

Pierre was respected and beloved by many, but he still faced prejudice and discrimination. He donated a large amount of money to help build the original Saint Patrick's Cathedral. On the day of the cathedral's dedication, Pierre went to the service. At first, he was not allowed to enter because he was Black. As he turned to leave, he was recognized and escorted to a seat of honor. Despite this suffering, Pierre was always happy to talk to anyone about his Catholic faith and God's love. He was known all over New York for his kindness, his wisdom, and his faith, and is considered one of the founders of Catholic charitable works in the United States.

Pierre had some choices. He could have abandoned Berard's widow and his friends. With all his money, he could have retired and lived an easy life of luxury ignoring those less fortunate. Instead, he chose to work hard and to love and serve anyone in need, because they were all God's children. He chose to live his faith proudly in a time when the Catholic Faith was ridiculed. Who would have thought that styling hair could make such a difference in so many people's lives? Pierre used every opportunity to evangelize and tell people about God's love. He supported and encouraged his fellow Catholics. What choices have you made? Are you generous and giving? Work hard, keep your dignity, help others, and stand for your faith. Be like Pierre and choose to be like Christ!

28
PATRICK

The Firebringer

*Once a slave, he returned to the land of his
captivity and converted a nation.*

Patrick was born in Britain in 387. When he was a teenager, Patrick was captured by Irish pirates. He was sold as a slave to a chieftain in Ireland and was put to work taking care of the chieftain's sheep. Patrick was cold, hungry, and scared. He was in a strange land with strange people. So he did what he had been taught as a child to do when he got scared: He prayed. The more he prayed, the less scared he felt. The more he prayed, the closer he got to God. When he wrote about this time, he said, "More and more did the love of God, and my fear of him and faith increase, and my spirit was moved so that in a day [I said] from one up to a hundred prayers, and in the night a like number; besides I used to stay out in the forests and on the mountain and I would wake up before daylight to pray in the snow, in icy coldness, in rain, and I used to feel neither ill nor any slothfulness, because, as I now see, the Spirit was burning in me at that time."

After six years, Patrick heard a voice in a dream. The voice told him that there would be a ship two hundred miles away that could take him home. Patrick ran from his master. He walked the long miles and found the boat right where the voice had told him it would be. When

> **PATRICK SAID:**
> "I fear nothing, because of the promises of heaven; for I have cast myself into the hands of Almighty God, who reigns everywhere. As the prophet says: 'Cast your burden on the Lord and he will sustain you.'"

SAINT

FULL NAME:
Patrick of Ireland

N NICKNAME:
The Firebringer

Y YEARS: 387–461

C COUNTRY: Ireland

the captain refused to take him, Patrick fell to his knees and prayed until the captain changed his mind.

Patrick arrived home in Britain. His family was overjoyed to see him alive. They expected him to stay home with them, but God had other ideas. Soon Patrick was having dreams again. In a recurring dream, the people of Ireland were calling him to come back to them. Patrick decided this meant that he was to go back to Ireland and bring them the Catholic Faith. He became a priest and then a bishop, and eventually he was appointed to be the bishop of Ireland.

Patrick set about bringing the Faith to Ireland. He knew that it would be a tremendous help if he could get the High King Laoghaire, who ruled central Ireland, to support him. Laoghaire, however, wanted nothing to do with this new religion. He believed that the druids, the Celtic pagan priests, had all the power he needed.

The night before Easter, Laoghaire was having a celebration with the druids. It was a law that no one could light a fire until the druids lit their ceremonial fire. But on another hill, Patrick was celebrating the Easter Vigil, which always starts with the lighting of the Easter fire symbolizing the Light of Christ. Patrick lit a big Easter fire before the druids lit theirs. Laoghaire was furious. His druids told the king that if he didn't put out Patrick's fire, it would spread through all of Ireland. Laoghaire ordered his soldiers to take their chariots and go kill Patrick. When Patrick saw the chariots coming, he calmly prayed the words of Psalm 68:1, "Let God arise, let his enemies be scattered; let those who hate him flee before him!" A strong, dark whirlwind swirled around the soldiers. They fell to the ground in fear. Patrick's fire burned brighter than ever. Impressed with the power of Patrick's God, King Laoghaire allowed him to preach the Gospel of Jesus to the people. The druids' prediction came true, and the light of Christ spread throughout all of Ireland.

Patrick continued spreading the Gospel. He converted thousands of people. He founded hundreds of churches, performed miracles, and healed many people. He wrote a book telling of his experiences. By the time Patrick died, the Catholic Faith was strongly established in Ireland.

Patrick trusted God. He trusted him when he was a slave, and the Lord brought him home. Patrick trusted God when he lit the fire and was attacked, and the Lord saved him. God never let Patrick down. God was there when Patrick needed him, and God is there for you too! When you feel abandoned, lost, or scared, pray as Patrick did. Trust in God, and he will never let you down.

Next Saint Patrick's Day, along with wearing green and eating corned beef and cabbage, take a moment to think about Patrick. Patrick trusted God when he was called to be a priest and he converted a nation. You too can do great things when you trust in God. You too can be a Firebringer!

29
IGNATIUS

The Educator

He longed to be a knight and go on amazing adventures,
then he became a priest and changed the world!

In 1491, Ignatius of Loyola was born into a noble family of knights, soldiers, and adventurers (one of his brothers sailed with Columbus) in Azpeitia, Spain. Growing up, Ignatius wanted to be like his father and brothers. He longed to be a famous knight serving a great king to gain the favor of a beautiful lady. Unfortunately, Ignatius was quick to fight, had a bad gambling problem, was known for an immoral lifestyle, and killed several men in duels. He was more focused on looking good than being good.

Ignatius took a position as a soldier in the service of the Duke of Nájera. When France attacked Pamplona with heavy artillery and twelve thousand men, Ignatius and his men fought bravely despite the odds. To inspire his men, Ignatius stood at the fortress wall with his sword in hand. Suddenly he was struck in the legs by a cannonball. Ignatius fell to the ground and the battle was lost. One of Ignatius' legs had been shattered by the cannonball. The army doctors set his leg the best they could and sent him home. However, the bone was not properly set and so his leg looked rather ugly. Fond of his dashing appearance, Ignatius insisted that his leg needed to be rebroken and set again.

Ignatius had to stay in bed for a long time while his leg healed. He asked for books on his favorite topic, the gallant adventures of knights and their beautiful ladies. Having no other

> **IGNATIUS SAID:**
> "He who goes about to reform the world must begin with himself, or he loses his labor."

options, the bored Ignatius read the two books over and over. Ignatius began to think. What if he did what Saint Francis had done? What if he lived as those other inspiring saints? He still wanted to do great things, but now he was going to do them in the name of Christ, just like his new heroes. He would sacrifice and give his life in the service to the greatest King of all.

When he recovered, Ignatius traveled to Montserrat. He gave his clothes to a poor peasant and laid his sword at the altar of Our Lady of Montserrat. He then entered a Dominican friary and spent time in prayer and penance. He was filled with a sense of peace and decided that this peace came from doing the will of God. At this time, he started writing the *Spiritual Exercises*, a program of praying, examining one's conscience, imagining what it was like to be present at events in the Bible, and gaining peace by figuring out God's will for one's life. Ignatius left the friary and went on a pilgrimage to Jerusalem, visiting all the places Christ had lived and worked. During this pilgrimage, he decided that he would study so that he would be better prepared to help people come to Jesus. For twelve years, Ignatius studied at different universities. In Paris, he became a priest.

Ignatius formed a group of friends who would go out to take care of the sick and dying. Ignatius began preaching and teaching. Together with his college roommates (both of whom are now saints), he formed the Society of Jesus, also called the Jesuits. The group focused on serving the needs of God's people wherever and whenever they were needed. Along with the usual vows of poverty, chastity, and obedience, they made a fourth vow of obedience to the pope. They promised to accept whatever mission and go wherever the pope needed them to go. Ignatius felt that the members of the society needed to be well educated in order to serve well, so he made this a requirement.

The value of education inspired Ignatius and the Jesuits to found universities. By the end of the 1700s, there were more than 800 Jesuit high schools, colleges, and universities all over the world. Not only were the Jesuits involved in education, but they were also pioneers in science and exploration. By 1750, thirty of the world's 130 astronomical observatories were run by Jesuit astronomers, and thirty-five lunar craters have been named to honor Jesuit scientists. Europe's switch to the Gregorian calendar was the work of the Jesuit Christopher Clavius, who was considered one of the most influential teachers of the Renaissance. Jesuit scientist Athanasius Kircher was the first to discover that the bubonic plague was spread by microorganisms. Jesuits are still running observatories and making scientific discoveries today.

The Jesuits went out as missionaries all over the world. Among other accomplishments, Jesuit explorers founded cities, discovered the source of the Blue Nile river, and charted the Amazon and Mississippi rivers. Jesuit missionaries brought rhubarb, quinine, vanilla, and ginseng back from Asia and South America. They brought Jesus to the farthest regions of our earth.

By the time Ignatius died,

SAINT

FULL NAME:
Ignatius of Loyola

N **NICKNAME:**
The Educator

Y **YEARS:** 1491–1556

C **COUNTRY:** Spain

his Jesuits were well established and growing quickly. Today the Society of Jesus is the largest male religious order in the Catholic Church. With over 16,000 members, Jesuits are teachers, pastors, doctors, lawyers, scientists, and more!

At first, Ignatius had wanted to be a famous knight and change the world. Then he wanted to be just like the famous saints he read about. He became both. When Ignatius was sending his Jesuits off to the missions, he would encourage them by saying, "Go, set the world on fire!" Ignatius was inspired by reading about the lives of saints. What will reading about the life of Ignatius inspire you to do? Go, set the world on fire!

30
JOSÉ

Gaucho (Cowboy)

*With his sombrero and poncho, José looked just
like a cowboy, but under that sombrero was an
engineer and priest devoted to his people.*

José Gabriel del Rosario Brochero was born in 1840 in Santa Rosa, Argentina. He was one of ten children born to a good Catholic family. Both his sisters became nuns. When he was just sixteen years old, José decided to become a priest and entered the seminary. There he went through the *Spiritual Exercises*. The *Spiritual Exercises*, written by Ignatius, who you just read about in the last chapter, are a set of prayers and meditations to help people have a deeper relationship with God. José lived in Córdoba, where he was teaching at the seminary, and studying at the university. After being ordained, he was made the assistant pastor there. José spent much of his time going out into the worst sections of Córdoba to minister to the poor and ill, and became known for his compassion for the destitute of the city. When a cholera epidemic hit the city, José worked tirelessly, caring for the sick and dying.

While assigned to Córdoba, a railroad was built between Córdoba and Rosario. José saw the boost that this gave to the country people who lived between the two cities. He never forgot how it improved their lives. When he was twenty-nine years old, José was assigned to San Alberto's Parish. High in the mountains of Argentina, this parish was 1,675 square miles. The people were isolated from the rest of the country by the mountains.

JOSÉ SAID:
"Woe if the Devil is going
to rob a soul from me!"

SAINT

FULL NAME:
José Gabriel del
Rosario Brochero

N NICKNAME:
Gaucho (Cowboy)

Y YEARS: 1840–1914

C COUNTRY: Argentina

There were no roads and very little communication with the outside world. Because of this, they were very poor, both physically and spiritually. Their living conditions were terrible. As José said, "They have been abandoned by all, but not by God." José became determined to bring Jesus and the sacraments to these people, as well as improving their education and economic circumstances.

José did not spend all his time in the parish office. Instead, the priest was a familiar sight as he traveled around his huge parish on his faithful mule, ministering to his new people. Wearing his poncho and sombrero over his cassock, with a cigar hanging out of his mouth, he looked like a typical Argentinian cowboy. He became known as the *gaucho* (the Spanish word for cowboy) priest. José preached the Gospel using the native language of the people, Quechua, so it would be easier for them to understand. Remembering how the *Spiritual Exercises* had helped him grow in faith, he began to lead pilgrimages of people to Córdoba for retreats. For years, José led caravans of up to 500 people 125 miles — sometimes through deep snow — to spend nine days in prayer and meditation.

While the people were growing in faith, they began to change their lives. José remembered seeing how building the railway had helped the country people outside Córdoba. He and his parishioners began to build roads. They built over 125 miles of roads that are still known as Brocheriano roads after José. They built churches, villages, and schools. He convinced the authorities to put in telegraph systems and post offices. He planned a railway that eventually joined 200 miles of villages. He built Houses of Exercises where the *Spiritual Exercises* of Saint Ignatius could be taught, meaning that the people no longer had to make the long journey to Córdoba. More than 40,000 people went through the retreat during his time as their pastor.

Nothing stopped José from ministering to his people. Despite rain, snow, difficult roads, or no roads at all, José made sure that anyone needing the sacraments would get them. If anyone was in need, sick or dying, José rode to care for them. In one of the villages was a leper. Everyone was afraid of catching leprosy, so this man was abandoned. When José heard about the leper, he went to care for him, showing him God's love even though José knew that he could catch the disease.

José did end up catching leprosy and died in his home in Córdoba, cared for by his two sisters. His last words were, "Now I have everything ready for the journey." As Pope Francis said when he declared José the first Argentinian saint, "[José] was a shepherd who smelled of sheep, poor among the poor. He knew the love of Jesus. He let his heart be touched by the mercy of God, which he extended to all people. For the people of his parish, receiving a visit from him was like a visit from Jesus to each family."

José didn't just spend his time in his church or in his office. He went out to the people. He looked for ways to help improve their daily lives. A local 1887 article described José this way: "He practices the Gospel. Are you missing a carpenter? He's a carpenter. Are you missing a laborer? He's a laborer. He rolls up his cassock wherever he is, takes the shovel or hoe and opens a public road in fifteen days aided by his parishioners." Jose didn't waste time. He saw a need and he acted on it. He wanted to change the world around him for the better … and he did! He now looks to help others to do the same. Look for people in need. Help your mom carry the grocery bags. Shovel a neighbor's front porch after a snowstorm. Help grow a community garden. Pitch in to help whoever and whenever you can. Even if you're hot or cold or tired, keep at it until the job is done. José is at your side. Will you join God's cowboy and ride out to change your world?

31
PETER

The Rock

*A stubborn fisherman who doubted and disappointed,
yet became the "rock" on which Jesus built his Church.*

Peter was a hard-working fisherman named Simon when he first met Jesus. Their meeting happened after a long day of fishing. Peter was very frustrated at not having been able to catch any fish. Jesus asked Peter to go out into the lake again and cast his nets. Peter was skeptical, but agreed to try one more time. To his amazement, when the nets were pulled in, they were loaded with all kinds of fish. Jesus asked Peter and some of his companions to come with him. "Follow me, and I will make you fishers of men" (Mt 4:19). With this meeting, Peter's life was changed forever!

Peter agreed, left everything, and began to travel with Jesus. He watched Jesus perform many miracles. He watched as Jesus made the blind see and the lame walk. He saw Jesus feed over five thousand people with five loaves of bread and two fish. He saw Jesus raise people from the dead! Peter was chosen by Christ to be the leader of the apostles. One day Jesus asked his disciples who people were saying Jesus was. Then Jesus asked the disciples, "'But who do you say that I am?' Simon Peter replied, 'You are the Christ, the Son of the living God.' And Jesus answered him, 'Blessed are you, Simon Bar-Jona! For flesh and blood has not revealed this to you, but my Father who is in heaven. And I tell you, you are Peter, and on this rock I will build my Church, and the gates

> **PETER SAID:**
> "Lord, to whom shall we go? You have the words of eternal life; and we have believed, and have come to know, that you are the Holy One of God" (Jn 6:68).

of Hades shall not prevail against it. I will give you the keys of the kingdom of heaven, and whatever you bind on earth shall be bound in heaven, and whatever you loose on earth shall be loosed in heaven'" (Mt 16:15–20).

Peter was not perfect. Once the apostles were in the middle of the lake in a boat. A storm came up and they were scared. When they looked across the lake, they saw Jesus walking toward them on top of the water! When Peter asked if he could walk on water too, Jesus told him to come. Peter stepped out of the boat and for a minute was walking on the water. Then he took his eyes off of Jesus, got scared, and began to sink. Jesus came to him and helped him back into the boat.

On the night Jesus was arrested, Peter followed him. When he was recognized as one of Jesus' followers, Peter — afraid that he too would be arrested — said that he didn't know Jesus. He denied that he knew Jesus not once, but three times! He denied Jesus three times, even though the evening before he had promised Jesus that he would die rather than deny him. Afterward, Peter vowed never to betray Jesus again, and he never did.

After Jesus' resurrection, when the Holy Spirit came down upon them at Pentecost, Peter and the rest of the apostles were filled with courage and inspiration. Peter, as the leader, was the first to tell the crowds about the resurrection of Jesus. He was the first to heal the sick and perform miracles in the name of Jesus. Fearless and tireless, he worked to build the new Church.

Once he was arrested to be tried and executed. The night before his trial, an angel appeared in his cell, released him from his chains, and led him past the guards to freedom. He continued baptizing and teaching. Peter wrote letters that became part of the Bible and have been read at Mass for centuries. He traveled to many lands teaching about Jesus. He finally ended up in Rome. It was there that he was arrested by the Romans and was crucified. Peter asked to be crucified upside down because he didn't consider himself worthy of dying exactly like Jesus.

Peter ended up in Rome, which at that time was considered the center of the world. What better place for Peter to establish the new Church? (The current pope still lives in the Vatican in Rome.) Remember earlier when Jesus gave Peter the keys of the kingdom? Jesus told him that he was the rock that Jesus would build his Church on, and that whatever he bound on earth would be bound in heaven and whatever loosed here on earth will be loosed in heaven. By this act, Jesus made Peter the first pope. The pope is in charge of leading the Church on Earth until Christ returns to lead it himself! All other popes are called the "successors of Peter."

Through the inspiration of God, Peter settled the arguments and set rules, and everyone respected his decisions. The word *pope* comes from the Latin word *papa* which means "father." That's why you will hear the pope referred to as the Holy Father. The pope is the leader, the father of the whole Catholic Church. In an unbroken line, coming from Jesus first giving the keys to Peter, there have been 266 popes guiding and caring for the Catholic Church.

SAINT

FULL NAME: Peter

NICKNAME: The Rock

YEARS: 1– 64

COUNTRY: Israel, Rome

Peter was a simple hard-working fisherman. He made mistakes. He fell into the lake because he doubted. He denied Jesus at the moment that Jesus needed him most. He knew nothing about public speaking or teaching. Yet, through the power of the Holy Spirit, he went on to become a dynamic speaker, a worker of miracles, the first pope, and was Jesus' right-hand man in building the Catholic Church.

What can happen if you say yes to the call of Jesus? How will your life be changed? What will the Holy Spirit do for you? Peter is waiting to help you find out!

32
JOHN

The Bishop

*He left everything he knew to come to a new country and
became the bishop who cared only to serve the people.*

Born in 1811 in Bohemia (now the Czech Republic), John Neumann wanted to be a priest ever since he was a little kid. John studied hard. When he finished his studies, he was faced with a challenge: Bohemia had too many priests! Because there was nowhere to put the extra priests, the bishop refused to ordain any more.

John was determined. He heard that they needed priests in America, and contacted the bishop of New York. The bishop agreed to ordain him. Three weeks later, John was ordained and was sent to the parish of Buffalo. This parish included 900 square miles of territory. Working in such a large parish, John felt the need to join a community for support. He decided to join the Redemptorist order. The

JOHN SAID:
"We are not sent into this world for nothing; we are not born at random; we are not here, that we may go to bed at night and get up in the morning, til for our bread, eat and drink, laugh and joke, sin when we have a mind and reform when we are tired of sinning, rear a family, and die. God sees every one of us; He creates every soul … for a purpose. He needs, he deigns to need every one of us. He has an end for each of us; we are all equal in his sight, and we are placed in our different ranks and stations, not to get what we can out of them for ourselves, but to labor in them for him. As Christ has his work, we too have ours; as he rejoiced to do his work, we must rejoice in ours also."

SAINT

FULL NAME:
John Neumann

NICKNAME: The Bishop

YEARS: 1811–1860

COUNTRY:
Bohemia(Czech Republic),
United States

Redemptorists are dedicated to missionary work. John became a Redemptorist Father and later was made bishop of Philadelphia.

At that time, the diocese of Philadelphia covered a huge area. Two-thirds of Pennsylvania, all of Delaware, and western New Jersey were all under John's direction. He decided that he wanted to visit every parish, hospital, religious community, and orphanage in his diocese. John spent much of his time on horseback traveling across this huge area. He was only five feet and four inches tall, so his legs couldn't reach the stirrups and would stick out on either side of the horse, which often made people laugh. Climbing mountains, sleeping in barns, and saying Mass on kitchen tables, John worked hard serving his people. He avoided the pomp and ceremony usually given to bishops. Once on a visit, the local priest picked him up in a manure wagon. Instead of being offended, John joked, "Have you ever seen such an entourage for a bishop!" His clothes became tattered and he wore the same pair of boots for his whole time in Philadelphia. On one visit, when asked if he would like to change his boots, he replied with a smile, "The only way I could change my shoes is by putting the left one on the right foot and the right one on the left foot. This is the only pair I own."

In the eighty months he served as bishop, he built eighty new churches and forty new schools. John started the first unified parochial school system, boosting student attendance from 500 to 9,000! He loved meeting and ministering to the people. Because he was fluent in eight languages, he was able to speak with and hear the confessions of the many immigrants in his diocese.

There was a violent anti-Catholic movement in Philadelphia at this time. Two churches had already been burned to the ground. His priests, afraid that more activity would cause more violence, started advising John to lay low and not start anything new. However, John was in the middle of planning to start a Forty Hours devotion across the diocese. Forty Hours involves having a church open for forty hours in a row of Eucharistic adoration. John prayed to know what to do. One night, after working late by candlelight, John fell asleep at his desk. The candle burnt down and charred the papers he was reading. John woke up and was alarmed, but thankful that a big fire hadn't started. He could even still read the charred papers. He knelt to thank God. As he prayed, God spoke to him saying, "As the flames are burning here without consuming or injuring the writing, so shall I pour out my grace in the Blessed Sacrament without prejudice to my honor. Fear no profanation, therefore; hesitate no longer to carry out your design for my glory." John knew then that he had nothing to fear. He went on to introduce Forty Hours to the Philadelphia diocese. The devotion was eventually established in all of the United States and continues today.

John knew he had a mission. Without fear, he traveled to a new land. With enthusiasm, he endured miles on horseback, sleeping in haystacks, and even riding in a manure wagon in order to serve God's people. In the face of persecution and violence, he stood firm. He lived the Gospel with courage, energy, and humor.

Today there is still anti-Catholic prejudice. Priests, religious, and the Catholic Faith are often ridiculed publicly and privately. Churches are still being burned. In some lands, Catholics are still being killed for their faith. John knew what it was like to stand up for his faith. He did everything he could to promote and spread the truth. If someone makes fun of Catholics in front of you, do you have the courage to stand firm and stick up for your faith? Are you a champion for your faith, joyfully telling others about Jesus Christ? John would love to help you do just that. He is by your side to give you encouragement and courage!

33
AUGUSTINE

The Reformed

He tried very hard to not live a Christian life,
but ended up a Doctor of the Church!

Born in Thagaste, Africa, in 354, Augustine was the son of a pagan father and Christian mother. He was raised a Christian, but soon decided that Christian living was not for him. He and his friends once stole the pears from a neighbor's tree just to enjoy the thrill of stealing them. Then as he grew older and went off to the university, he and his friends became well known for their drinking, partying, and immoral living. Despite all his constant partying, Augustine still found time to study. He had a brilliant mind and enjoyed learning. After studying other religions, Augustine decided that he was definitely not a Christian and did not want to live a Christian life.

When he completed his studies, Augustine returned home. Unlike his brother and sister who both had entered religious life, Augustine was lazy and only interested in drinking and women. At one point, his mother Monica, reached her breaking point and refused to live with him. Shortly afterwards, Monica had a vision that Augustine would come back to the Faith, and so once again she agreed to live with him. But she continued praying and fasting all the time for his conversion. This really annoyed Augustine. He told his mother that he wanted to go to Rome to pursue his studies, but she begged him not to. So, Augustine told her he was going to the dock

> **AUGUSTINE SAID:**
> "Thou hast made us for thyself, O Lord, and our heart is restless until it finds its rest in thee."

SAINT

FULL NAME:
Augustine of Hippo

N **NICKNAME:**
The Reformed

Y **YEARS:** 354–430

C **COUNTRY:** Algeria, North Africa

to say goodbye to a friend — but instead, he hopped on a boat to Rome. When Monica found out what he had done, she was heart-broken, but eventually followed him to Rome. When she arrived in Rome, she found out that Augustine had gone on to Milan. She followed after him, praying as she went.

In Milan, everyone was talking about the dynamic preaching of a bishop named Ambrose (who himself became a saint). Augustine went to hear Ambrose preach, and was fascinated with what he said. He began studying with Ambrose and came to believe that Christianity was the one true religion. But because of all his sins and bad habits, he still didn't believe he could live a Christian life. He heard of two men who had converted simply by reading a biography of St. Anthony of the Desert. Augustine felt ashamed of how, after all his studying, and what he had come to realize as the truth, he was still not living a Christian life. He begged God to show him the way, and immediately heard a small child singing, "Pick it up and read." Augustine picked up a book of the letters of Saint Paul and read: "Let us conduct ourselves becomingly as in the day, not in reveling and drunkenness, not in debauchery and licentiousness, not in quarreling and jealousy. But put on the Lord Jesus Christ, and make no provision for the flesh, to gratify its desires" (Rom 13:13–14). That was the answer!

Augustine began a new life. He was baptized a Christian, which made his mom, Monica (who became a saint), very, very happy! Augustine went on to be ordained a priest and eventually became the bishop of Hippo, a city on the coast of North Africa. He founded a religious order and became known for his great faith and charitable good works. He was a great preacher and converted thousands. Augustine wrote a book telling the story of his journey from wild child to faithful Christian called *The Confessions*. This honest sharing of his mistakes, emotions, and conversion shocked and inspired the readers of his day, and continues to inspire people today. Augustine also wrote detailed explanations of the Faith. These writings were so influential and valued that, after his death, Augustine was declared a Doctor of the Church.

Toward the end of his life, Augustine exclaimed to God, "Late have I loved you, beauty so ancient and so new!" He began his life without God, trying to find fulfillment in all the wrong places. But when he saw the truth, he made up for all his mistakes and used those same mistakes to bring people to God. No matter what you've done in the past, God still loves you. He made you for a purpose and can bring good out of even the worst experience. If you keep turning to him for help, he will always be there for you. If you are willing, he will make you a force for good in the world. Augustine will be right there cheering you on!

34
JEROME

Champion of the Unborn

*Known as the father of modern genetics, he gave up wealth
and fame to champion those who have no voice.*

Jerome Lejeune was born in 1926 in Montrouge, a suburb of Paris, France. Wanting to help people, he grew up to study medicine and become a doctor. In 1952, he married the love of his life, Birthe Bringsted. Birthe loved her husband very much and wanted to share his faith, so she converted to Catholicism. Together they had five children who were all baptized Catholic.

Jerome was a skilled medical researcher, and in 1958, he discovered the gene for Down syndrome. Children born with this condition have different degrees of intellectual and physical delays and disabilities. Jerome hoped that his discovery would help treat Down syndrome children. Instead, ten years after his discovery, doctors began using Jerome's methods of prenatal diagnosis to find out if a pregnant woman was having a child with Down syndrome or some other chromosomal abnormality. If they found out the child would have Down syndrome, often the child would be aborted. Abortion is a medical procedure that kills a baby while the baby is still in his or her mother.

After his discovery, Jerome was a famous, admired scientist. Jerome spoke at thousands of medical conferences. Then he was given the William Allen Award, the highest award given for work in genetics. This was

JEROME SAID:
"We need to be clear: The quality of a civilization can be measured by the respect it has for its weakest members. There is no other criterion."

about the time that his discovery had started being used to diagnose disabilities and perform abortions. A faithful Catholic who had to speak his conscience, Jerome used this huge platform to speak out against abortion, even though he knew that he would be ridiculed for it. Jerome's daughter wrote in her book *Life is a Blessing* of what happened to her father when he started speaking out against abortion: "Here is a man who, because his convictions as a physician prohibited him from following the trends of his time, was banned by society, dropped by his friends, humiliated, crucified by the press, prevented from working for lack of funding. Here was a man who became, for certain people, a man to be beaten down; for others, a man not worth jeopardizing your reputation with; and for still others, an incompetent extremist."

The ridicule only made Jerome a more outspoken opponent of abortion. He spoke out against those who would treat his "little ones" — as he called his Down syndrome patients — not as people but as problems that should be prevented. Already a member of the Pontifical Academy of Sciences, Jerome was called upon to help found the Pontifical Academy for Life by Pope Saint John Paul II. Until Jerome's death in 1994, he continued to do chromosomal research, always aimed at helping and curing. He especially focused on helping those with Down syndrome. He never gave up crusading for life and the dignity of every person, no matter how tiny.

Even after his death, his crusade went on. Before he died, Jerome told his children "not to worry," since they would see "how strong and full of capacity your mom is." He was right. Birthe carried on Jerome's work. A year after his death, she helped found The Jerome Lejeune Foundation in his memory. The foundation focuses on researching, treating, and defending those with Down syndrome and intellectual disabilities of genetic origin. At Birthe's funeral, one of their 28 grandchildren, Emma Lejeune, said, "Grandpa was a brilliant scientist, but he was also very scatterbrained; while Grandma was extremely concrete, efficient and organized, and she could help him achieve things he might not have achieved without her." Together Birthe and Jerome had made it their life's work to help and speak for the most vulnerable of persons and had made a difference.

Today you hear a lot of people say that a woman should choose what's right for her body and be able to abort her baby if she so chooses. A guy might think that it is none of his business. But it is everyone's business! A woman does have a right to do whatever she wants with *her* body, but the baby growing inside her has his or her own little body, with his or her own little heartbeat. What is growing inside a pregnant mother is more than just a bunch of cells. It is a baby, a gift from God. That child's appearance, talents, and unique traits are present already in that tiny bundle of joy. Each child has a right to be born and have a life no matter what. Today millions of little ones are being killed every year because they are inconvenient or might have a disability. Someone has to fight for them!

SERVANT OF GOD

FULL NAME:
Jerome LeJeune

NICKNAME: Champion of the Unborn

YEARS: 1926–1994

COUNTRY: France

Jerome knew that every life has value and purpose. He fought for those little ones who have no voice. He said, "The reality of it is that, by caring for the weak, by caring for the most vulnerable, we are made strong. So if we can launch this project caring for the weakest, we are made stronger. If we are made stronger, we can advocate better." Now Jerome asks you to stand up and fight for the vulnerable. Everyone's life has value and dignity no matter what. He needs you to bring help, care, and respect to those who have any kind of disability. He needs you to fight for the unborn, for those who have no voice. Will you be their champion?

35
JOSEPH

Ultimate Guardian

None of his words are written in the Bible, and he
doesn't get half of the attention his wife gets. Yet no man
on earth was ever given a more important job.

The Bible doesn't tell us too much about Joseph. In the Bible, we first meet Joseph when he is betrothed to Mary. In those days, when a couple was betrothed, it was a kind of legally binding engagement. After Mary was visited by the Angel Gabriel and became pregnant through the power of the Holy Spirit, this became a challenge for Joseph. Joseph was worried and confused that his wife was having a baby before they were married. But Joseph was a good man. He thought he had to break off the betrothal, but wanted to do it as quietly as possible so as to prevent Mary from being ridiculed. But then, an angel came to him in a dream and told him not to be afraid to take Mary as his wife. The angel told Joseph that the child Mary carried was the Son of God who would redeem the world. God wanted Joseph to care for and protect Mary and her Son.

The Bible also says that Joseph was a just and righteous man. That means Joseph was a man of faith and obedient to God. Like Mary, Joseph said yes to God and helped change the world by agreeing to be the guardian of God on earth.

> **SAINT TERESA OF ÁVILA SAID OF JOSEPH:**
> "To other saints, the Lord seems to have given grace to help us in some of our necessities. But my experience is that Saint Joseph helps us in them all; also that the Lord wishes to teach us that, as he was himself subject on earth to Saint Joseph, so in heaven, he now does all that Joseph asks."

Joseph trusted God's will and married Mary. He took Mary to Beth-lehem, where the baby Jesus was born. He marveled at the wise men and shepherds who came to adore the child. The wise men had followed the star to find the great king who had just been born. On their way, they had stopped to ask King Herod if he knew where the newborn king was. King Herod became furiously jealous of this new king, and was determined to find the baby and kill him. After Joseph and Mary had presented the baby Jesus in the Temple, Joseph had another dream. In the dream, an angel told Joseph to get up immediately and take Jesus and his mother to Egypt. The angel said that Herod was searching for the child so he could murder Jesus.

Again that just man, Joseph, did exactly what God asked. He woke Mary and they quickly gathered everything they could carry and fled as fast as they could to Egypt. It took courage to make a life in a whole new country, and Joseph worked hard to support and protect Mary and little Jesus the very best he could. After several long years, the angel told Joseph that Herod had died and it was safe to return to Israel.

Joseph settled his family back in Nazareth. The Bible tells us that Joseph was a craftsman and probably worked with wood. Joseph would have taught these skills to the young Jesus. As Jesus got older, he most likely would have been a helper for his foster father and gone with Joseph to help him on his jobs. The two were probably a familiar sight traveling around to the different houses in Nazareth to put in a door, repair a roof, or whatever was needed. This is probably why the Bible says that when Jesus started preaching and performing miracles, the people of his hometown wouldn't accept him. They knew him as the carpenter's son, who had come to their houses with his father to fix stuff!

The only other time you hear about Joseph in the Bible was when he, Mary, and Jesus traveled to Jerusalem when Jesus was twelve. They went there for the Festival of the Passover with a large group of family and friends. On the way home, Joseph and Mary assumed Jesus was hang-ing out with his friends or with relatives, so they didn't worry when they didn't see him, but finally they noticed that he was missing. After fran-tically searching everywhere among their caravan, they headed back to Jerusalem. Can you imagine what Joseph was feeling? He was supposed to take care of the Son of God, and Jesus was lost somewhere in the big city of

Jerusalem! He and Mary desperately searched, until three days later they discovered Jesus in the Temple, calmly discussing religion with the elders. After seeing how upset Mary and Joseph were, Jesus said: "How is it that you sought me? Did you not know that I must be in my Father's house?" (Lk 2:49). The Bible said that after this happened, Jesus returned to Nazareth with Mary and Joseph and was obedient to them.

Joseph was trusted by God to be the foster father of Jesus and take care of him and his mother. He did his very best to lovingly care for all of their needs. Luckily for us, he still does that for those who come to him for help today. Jesus loves and respects his foster father and still lis-

SAINT

FULL NAME:
Joseph

N NICKNAME:
The Ultimate Guardian

Y YEARS: Unknown B.C.
– around 18 A.D.

C COUNTRY: Israel

tens to Joseph when he asks. During the Middle Ages, there were many cases of people and families (and even an entire city!) being saved from the plague by praying to Saint Joseph. Because he was a hard worker, Joseph is also a friend to workers and those looking for work.

If someone is sick or having trouble, put them in Joseph's care. If someone is having trouble at work or needs a job, ask Joseph to talk to his foster son, Jesus. If a dangerous sickness is going around, ask Joseph for his protection. He is the Ultimate Guardian!

And don't forget to do what you should do: be a just person, like Joseph!

36
FRANZ

The Motorcycle Martyr

He was a gang leader, troublemaker, motorcycle enthusiast, and conscientious objector who became a martyr for the Faith!

Franz Jagerstatter was born in Sankt Radegund, Austria, the son of an unwed mother. He started out as a troublemaker. He grew up to love riding motorcycles and soon became the leader of a gang that was known for drinking, immorality, and fighting. They were often in trouble with the police. Things got so bad that Franz was thrown out of the local community for several years.

Franz continued to get in trouble until he fell in love with and married Franziska Schwaninger. They had three daughters together and attempted to adopt the illegitimate daughter Franz had from a previous relationship. Franziska was a faithful Catholic and soon influenced her wild husband to start going to church again. Franz began to study the lives of the saints. He read the Bible daily, and tried to memorize as many verses as possible. Franz became a farmer. He was so happy in his new life that he told his wife, "I could have never imagined that being married could be so wonderful."

It wasn't a happy time for Austria though. The Nazi army of Hitler's Germany had just invaded. The Nazis believed in National Socialism, which glo-

> **FRANZ SAID:**
> "Since the death of Christ, almost every century has seen the persecution of Christians; there have always been heroes and martyrs who gave their lives — often in horrible ways — for Christ and their faith. If we hope to reach our goal some day, then we, too, must become heroes of the Faith."

rified war and so-called racial purity. The Catholic Church had been warning the people for years about the Nazis and their policies. Franz's pastor had been arrested for giving an anti-Nazi speech. His bishop had declared that "it is impossible to be a good Catholic and a true Nazi. The Nazi standpoint on race is completely incompatible with Christianity and must, therefore, be resolutely rejected. To despise, hate, and persecute the Jewish people just because of their ancestry is inhuman and against Christian principles."

As word spread of the Jewish people being persecuted and killed, Franz decided that he had to speak up against the Nazis. He spoke to friends, neighbors, city, and church officials. He told them of his resolution to never fight for this evil regime. After the Nazis invaded, Hitler held a vote on whether Austria should become part of Germany; 99.7 percent of the Austrian people voted in favor. Franz was part of the tiny percentage that voted no. In fact, he was the only one in his town who voted no.

As Franz's faith deepened, he decided to join the Franciscan Order as a lay member. He grew even more determined to be a sign to others that "not everyone let themselves be carried away with the tide." As the need for more German soldiers grew, Franz was drafted into the army and then called to active duty. He reported to the induction center, but refused to take the oath of loyalty to Hitler. For this, he was arrested and put in prison. Friends and family came to visit him in prison, trying to get him to change his mind. His lawyer pointed out that other Catholics were serving in the army. Franz replied, "I can only act on my own conscience. I do not judge anyone. I can only judge myself." His friends urged him to consider the effects of his choice on his family. Franz told them, "I have considered my family. I have prayed and put myself and my family in God's hands. I know that, if I do what I think God wants me to do, he will take care of my family."

Franziska, knowing how strong her husband's convictions were, supported his decision. Franz wrote her letters while in prison. Afraid that she too would be arrested, Franziska hid the letters until after the war. His last letter was written in Berlin, Germany. He had been taken there to stand trial for sedition (rebelling against the Nazis). He thanked

Franziska for her strength, support, and love. Franz then asked her forgiveness for all the pain and worry his actions and arrest had caused her, and for leaving her alone with their girls. He promised to "beg the dear God if I am permitted to enter heaven soon, that he will set aside a little place in heaven for all of you."

The day after Franz wrote those words, he was found guilty of sedition and beheaded. He was beatified fifty years later. The ceremony was attended by his daughters, grandchildren, and great-grandchildren. In honor of her husband, his ninety-four-year-old widow, Franziska, rode to the beatification in the sidecar of a motorcycle.

BLESSED

FULL NAME:
Franz Jagerstatter

N NICKNAME: The Motorcycle Martyr

Y YEARS: 1907–1943

C COUNTRY: Austria

Franz gave his life for what he believed in. Could you do it? Give up everything for Christ? Hopefully, you won't ever have to make the ultimate sacrifice as Franz did, but it's something to think about. People are standing for their Christian beliefs and giving their lives even today. Do you have the bravery of Franz to stand up and declare, "I am a Christian! This is what I believe in!"?

The Challenge

Do you have the courage to live your life as a Catholic? Can you make the right choice even when it is the hard choice? Are you willing to show, through your actions and words, that you are a Christian, even though you might face ridicule or persecution? Will you live the Gospel even when it seems impossible? Will you stand bravely and unflinchingly against prejudice and injustice? Will you be a voice for the voiceless and a help for the needy? Will you use every opportunity, no matter how small, to be a force for good and fight against the darkness? God is asking you to join his team of superheroes. All the men in this book are at your side. Jesus is with you. Go make a difference in the world!

JESUS SAID:
"You are the light of the world!"

IMPORTANT WORDS

Bilocation — The miraculous God-given ability of a holy person to appear in two places at one time.

Doctor of the Church — A title given to a saint whose writings and influence have been especially important and helpful to the Catholic Faith and people.

Doctrine — A truth revealed by God through Scripture or Tradition and held and taught by the Church.

Habit — The identifying outfit worn by a particular religious order.

Heretic — A baptized member of the Catholic Church who chooses to deny the truths of the Catholic Faith.

Intercession — The act of saying a prayer for another person.

Layperson — A member of the Church who is not a priest or religious.

Levitation — The ability of some very holy people to be so filled with the very presence of God that God suspends the rule of gravity and allows them to rise into the air.

Monk/friar/religious brother — A member of a religious community of men living their life dedicated to God, living under specific vows, typically poverty, chastity, and obedience.

Stigmata — The supernatural appearance of some or all of Jesus' crucifixion wounds on a person's hands, feet, side, and head.

Third Order — Lay members of a religious order who do the good works and follow the rule and spirit of that order, but are not formally professed and do not live in a community.

Vision — The supernatural appearances of something or someone, often of Jesus, Mary, saints, or angels, to a person chosen by God. A vision can occur while the person is awake or dreaming, and often God gives the person a vision because he wishes to convey some message.

ACKNOWLEDGMENTS

To God be the glory!

Thanks to everyone on the OSV team who helped me so much. Special thanks to Mary Beth for all her help and encouragement, and to Rebecca, my amazing, hard-working editor, whose inspired insight and suggestions were invaluable.

A special thank you to my original proofreaders — my father George Fluhr, my daughter Evangeline Bajda, and my dear friend Renate Muller, who gave so generously of their time and talent to give me valuable, honest input that helped me see what would and wouldn't work!

One's journey is shaped and influenced by all those one meets on the way. A huge thank you to all those wonderful priests and friends who inspired me with their faith, example, teachings, and support. My life and path would not be the same without you.

I also have to thank my beautiful, brave, talented, funny, loving children, James, Evangeline, and Isabelle, who put up with all those hours of me sitting at the computer being constantly distracted and forgetful. Their support, love, and humor inspire me and keep me going!

And of course, thank you to my biggest fan, my husband Jimi. He makes me laugh, holds me up, takes me for lunch and to the seashore, and paints stars on my ceiling. God gave me my best friend and the love of my life that New Year's Eve, and I am forever grateful!

Finally, my eternal thanks to the amazing superheroes I met on this journey. I am inspired by and in awe of your lives and faith. You have become my dear friends who inspire, motivate, and comfort me always. I hope I did you justice!

About the Author

Mary Fluhr Bajda loves her faith, family, music, and books. A graduate of Marywood University, she keeps busy as director of religious education and director of music and liturgy at Saint Ann's Church in Shohola, Pennsylvania, where she works with children of all ages. Her love of books, her interest in the saints, and her desire to help young people find their mission in the Catholic Church come together in her books. Mary enjoys country life with her family in the beautiful Pocono Mountains. She can be contacted at marybajda@gmail.com.

About the Illustrator

Melinda Steffen has been drawing ever since she was little. A lifelong Catholic originally from Livonia, Michigan, she has been a freelance illustrator in Brooklyn, New York, for over a decade. Under the name Mindy Indy, she creates her own comic series, *Aer Head*, and custom comic wall art. She can be contacted at mindy@mindyindy.com.